Reviewer's Comments

From <u>The Mountain Astrologer,</u> Dec 2012-Jan 2013

..."In this stunningly brilliant book, Beversdorf shows how you can design your own astrological prescriptions.... What makes [Vedic Secrets] so remarkable is that you don't have to be a Vedic Astrologer to experiment with these techniques.... Whether you've been reading charts your whole life or are a complete beginner, there's a treasure trove of eminently useful astrological lore here.... Vedic Secrets to Happiness is one of the most exciting astrology books I've seen in years. It could revolutionize the way astrology is practiced in the West by returning it to its ancient roots."

(reviewed by Linda Johnsen)

From Astrology Center of America Newsletter,

... I've got half a dozen books of remedies. Most of them are **dull** and full of gibberish. Many years ago Anne scraped up the money for **pujas** and to her surprise and delight, found they actually worked, curing her of depression. Encouraged, she started prescribing simple remedies for her friends and, to their surprise, they worked. After many years' experience, she wrote this book. The heart of it is planetary assessments. Go through them until you find the planet that hurts, and then go to the remedies section for that planet. There's a variety of remedies, some of them quite dazzling. Is your Mars giving you problems? Throw cinnamon red-hots into a stream on Tuesday. Saturn got you down? Listen to Requiem music on Saturdays! I can do that!

----David Roell, Astrology Center of America

The true role of Vedic astrology is not just to let people know "how" the planets are operating in their horoscopes, or even to let them know "when" the planets are operating in their horoscopes. Rather, it is to let them know "what" they can do as remedial measures to improve the quality of their lives.

To this end... **Vedic Secrets to Happiness** has accomplished a great deal. Read it, and most importantly, employ the planetary remedies for your own horoscope, for smoother sailing in life.

----David Hawthorne, Astroview, Inc.

NOW AVAILABLE!
Smartphone APP and PDF support.

"HAPPINESS VEDIC KEYS" is a new APP based on principles of this book. It can provide a quick reminder of activities you can perform to increase your life's happiness. Now available for your smartphone, so check your APP store.

Additional copies of this book's questionnaire are available in PDF form, in response to readers who are re-using them for regular life tune-ups. The PDFs are available at www.stariel.com/starielpress for a small fee.

VEDIC SECRETS TO HAPPINESS:

Life's Handbook

DEDICATION

With love, to Mom and Joe and William.

VEDIC SECRETS
TO HAPPINESS:

Life's Handbook

Anne Beversdorf

To Help You
Improve Life's Good Stuff
and
Reduce the Messes

Stariel Press

Stariel Press

Austin, Texas
www.stariel.com
StarielPress@stariel.com

CONTENTS

ILLUSTRATIONS

Illustration 1

Ganesha

SILK TAPESTRY BY ANNE BEVERSDORF

Honoring Ganesha, the elephant-headed god who removes
all obstacles to success.

Color image may be viewed at:
http://www.sacred-threads.com/tapestries-2/hindu-moslem-
images/ganesha/

PREFACE

We think of our modern world as technologically advanced, and certainly it is. We measure our comfort in computers, cars, airplanes, and smartphones. Yet, when it comes to technologies of another sort, it seems we are not so advanced. It would be difficult to say we are any happier or lead more contented lives than our predecessors did in the distant past. While our physical comfort and health may be better, I don't believe the world is populated with billions of people living deeply satisfying lives.

The cultural and religious traditions of India, which I'll refer to as *the Vedic tradition*, are being gradually rediscovered and integrated into many aspects of world culture. No longer does yoga seem exotic. Words like *karma*, and *mantra* and *pundit* are in common usage. *Meditation* is synonymous with deep inner silence and peace. Increasingly the deeper aspects of this tradition are being revived and adapted to fit our modern world.

The Vedic tradition draws a distinction between spirituality and religion. Spirituality implies feeding the spirit with methods that can be added to any life in order to bring deeper meaning, greater satisfaction, and inner peace to an individual. These methods are universal – applicable to any individual without any conflict with the religion and God they worship.

What Anne has accomplished here is unique. She has taken the disparate and scattered techniques from this broad cultural resource, and has refined and organized them so that they are useful, practical, and immediately accessible to anyone, regardless of how little or much they know about Vedic traditions.

Any person can pick up this book, follow the self-analysis, and select a series of practices to bring balance and peace into their lives. What could be simpler?

Yes, it *is* simple; yet, at the same time, it is up to you to take action. This is no quick process: neither is it a magical way to change your life in the blink of an eye. It is real, and it is work too. It is also a joyful and deeply meaningful art. You are embarking on the art of living!

This is a journey of inner and outer discovery that will bring you insight into the connectedness of the universe and your place in it. Let's get started!

Ben Collins, Founder
PUJA.NET
March 2012

INTRODUCTION:
THE MOST IMPORTANT CHAPTER

HOW TO USE THIS BOOK

When I read books like this, I usually get very excited and swear I'm going to do the activities and change my life. The problem is, I always bite off more than I can chew: I think if trying one thing is good I should add ten or twelve more, and by the time I figure out which ten or twelve activities I like, I'm so overwhelmed that nothing at all happens.

This book allows you to understand the various Energy Systems at work in your life and to diagnose which ones need balancing and support. When you learn which ones they are and what to do about it, your life will get easier and more fun.

First, you'll have a chance to diagnose your personal energy imbalances. Once you make the diagnosis, read the introduction to *Part III: Balancing Energies* (page 107). Then ...

**GO DIRECTLY TO BALANCING THE ENERGY SYSTEM
YOU'VE IDENTIFIED**

1

and
Scan the range of Balancing Activities.

The lists of Balancing Activities are the meat of this system. After you assess the Energy System you need to balance and find that activity list, then your job is to:

START SMALL!!

QUICKLY CHOOSE <u>ONE</u> ACTIVITY--

one that seems easiest and most natural.

MAKE PLANS TO BEGIN THAT ACTIVITY

on the first appropriate weekday.

CLOSE THE BOOK.

That's the beginning. You can always add more later. Yes, more is better, but doing something small immediately is better than hatching big intentions that never fly. I want this to work for you, so start easy and start small!

If you are attracted to this work and decide later to learn more, I suggest you contact a professional Jyotishi (Vedic astrologer) to fine-tune a "prescription" based on your personal birth information. This can add a whole new layer of assistance for you.

My one caution with this recommendation is that many Jyotishis habitually prescribe gemstones as remedies. Gemstone remedies should be used sparingly and intelligently. It sounds easy: all you have to do is buy one.

However, gemstones can cause harm in some areas of your life just as they can improve others, because they increase the specific energy field for good AND for ill. Furthermore, with gems, "you can't take it with you" after death. It's far better to use the life-improving activities of charity, service, ritual, *mantras*, *pujas*, and creative homage presented in this book. Doing so brings lasting change to your karma and you will avoid collateral damage.

I have been warned that offering remedies to people could cause me to take on the karma of anyone who either uses or misuses the remedies. I pray this is not the case. Even if it is, my feeling in *this* lifetime is that I am happy to do whatever will help others. We're all seeking the same goal and we won't reach it until we all get there. Of course, in some future lifetime I may be saying "WHAT WAS I THINKING?!" I'll take that chance.

PART I:

How I Found This

and

How It Works

Illustration 2

Release from Despair

SILK TAPESTRY BY ANNE BEVERSDORF
Based on a vision of HILDEGARD VON BINGEN.

Hildegard explains that the sword of divine grace
sweeps through the center,
shattering the heavy bricks of despair (on right)
making them fly away,
as light as feathers (on left).

Color image may be viewed at:
http://www.sacred-threads.com/tapestries-2/hildegard-von-bingen-
inspired/release-from-despair/

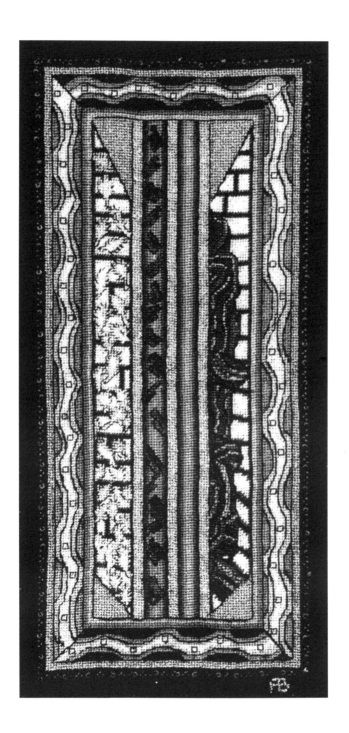

"Release from Despair"

1. DISCOVERY

This book can literally change your life. I would not have made such a claim years ago, yet I have now studied this system for two decades and the process works. The results continue to astonish me.

The basic premise: twelve major Energy Systems (and more) are at work in our lives, and sometimes these systems are out of balance with each other. You can understand how, if the Energy System of "discipline" is out of balance, you may experience extremes of punishment, or be too punitive with others, or maybe your life lacks discipline entirely. Alternatively, if the Energy System of "optimism and generosity" is off balance, you might overspend in the present, and assume your credit card debt doesn't matter.

The Vedas of Indian philosophical thought address many ways of balancing Energy Systems. The Sanskrit word "*Veda*" literally means *knowledge.* Ayurveda addresses issues of physical health. Jyotish, "the science of light", is the sixth limb of the Vedas and addresses subtle Energy Systems associated with the planets in our solar system. It was when I first studied Jyotish years ago that I encountered the systems you will read about in the following chapters.

At that time, I was learning how to understand an individual's life with Jyotish, which is the astrological limb of Vedic wisdom. I read an article that explained *upayas*, or "remedies," for out-of-balance energies. It is possible to have certain ceremonies performed, called *pujas* and *yagyas*, which rebalance these energies. These are arranged much as a Catholic will arrange to have a mass said. Each *puja* or *yagya* is designed to address a different Energy System. When I learned about *pujas* and *yagyas* there were few places a westerner could go for these services and the cost range was $5,000 to $50,000 per ceremony. I remember thinking,

> Boy, is THIS a scam! You tell someone they've got a problem and then charge them thousands to 'fix' it? You can get the same offer for less from the "Gypsy" palm reader next to the "massage" parlor.

To put it mildly, the "fix" didn't sit well with me. Despite that, I tucked the concept away and continued my studies.

Some time later I learned that the Indian saint, Ammaji, also offered *upayas* for planetary imbalances. Her organization only charged $35 per planetary energy system. This was affordable, and it just so happened that I had an imbalance to test.

For most of my adult life, I have been hit by periodic episodes of deep, dark, depression: the kind of depression where the world goes grey; colors cease to exist; and it takes all the energy in your soul just to get out of bed. It's a bleak way to live and I wanted it to stop. For whatever reason, I didn't want to use western drugs to address the problem. Because it was episodic, (with spells lasting up to five years), I kept thinking the depression would go away if I found the right herbs, or brain-training, or self-discipline, or whatever might show up. This seemed like an issue I could test with *upayas*.

First, I identified the Energy Systems that contributed to depression in my life. There were quite a few. Then I filled out the form and sent $140 to the Ammaji nonprofit group at www.amma.org, requesting ceremonies to balance the four unbalanced energies I identified.

~~~

One thing I have realized about Vedic thought is that this tradition is the original spiritual technology. The wisdom tradition of the Vedas goes back as far as 12,000 years in oral traditions, though it was only documented in the middle ages. Indian sages still teach Sanskrit scriptures to their students and children from the time they first utter syllables. Instead of learning nursery rhymes, the children of priests learn to parrot Vedic wisdom long before they can understand the words. We know the antiquity of Vedic tradition by matching geographic references in the Vedas to the geography and geology of the Indian continent over the past 12,000 years. This is ancient stuff.

Even today, East Indian priests can recite from memory thousands of pages of Sanskrit wisdom. The experts -- the sages and priests of India -- literally know the technology of using intention, prayer, sound, energy correspondences and the rules of energy harmonies to change things in the physical world. They know how to orchestrate space and time to encourage rain or prevent disasters, and they also know their limits. This is why I call this knowledge system *"spiritual technology"* rather than *"religion."* Hinduism seems alone among world religions in that it willingly accepts and absorbs the wisdom of all world teachers. At its core, Hinduism doesn't judge between those who follow one teacher and those who follow another. Of course, historical conquests and social patterns have created religious prejudice among some Hindus, just as they have in other religions.

~~~

So, back to my experiment: I justified the expenditure by telling myself,

> IF I am to practice Jyotish, the science of light, where the balance of energies can be seen to influence a person's life, and

> IF this is something traditional Jyotishis recommend,

> THEN I must find out for myself whether to recommend or discourage it as part of my practice.

After receiving my request and payment, the Ammaji organization of monks and priests in India would perform the ceremonies for the four Energy Systems I identified. Then they would mail me *prasad* -- parts of materials used in the ceremonies. Other ceremonial items, mainly foods, are given to the poor in their area. I didn't know when these ceremonies would take place or when my package of *prasad* would arrive, so I simply waited. While waiting I dragged myself out of bed, sat paralyzed all day while enjoining myself to DO SOMETHING, then dropped back into bed at night. Occasionally I managed to do something productive—when there was no other option.

On one particular day, I had a business meeting downtown. I was living in North County San Diego, which meant a long drive into the city. I gathered my courage and my remaining energy, dressed professionally, and drove to the meeting. Though it went reasonably well, as I drove home I began the process of "crashing".

For those of you lucky enough never to have experienced depression, I will explain "*crashing*" After pulling together every last drop of energy to accomplish something, once it's completed your body/mind/spirit want only to collapse—preferably minimally conscious, as in sleeping or staring at the wall. Such a drop happened on my drive home: I could feel myself falling. Then, to my utter surprise, at the halfway point, I hit what felt like a steel floor! I stopped falling. My new "resting" point was conscious, alert, and with energy reserves.

I was so shocked that I took a deep breath and (I'm embarrassed to say) tried again to collapse. I still couldn't do it! On a scale of 1 to 10, if rock bottom was zero before, now it was five: a position from which I could at least look around and see the world.

About ten days later, my package arrived from India. There was no indication of the date of the ceremonies, though my guess is that I reacted shortly after the ceremonies were complete, setting the stage for me to retrain myself into a healthier and happier pattern.

The new process continued. For months, the steel floor held solid. After four months, it became permeable, meaning that if I were unusually exhausted and tried hard, I could still crumple. Yet I didn't have to, I didn't want to, and furthermore, I had retrained myself to stop the fall at a healthier stage.

Now I owned personal evidence. I knew this energy technology worked.

2. LEARNING MORE:

EXPERIMENTS AND EXAMPLES

Now, realizing that *upayas* were not some bunco scam, I began a serious study of the systems involved. Through the work of K.N. Rao I learned that there are more ways of correcting energy than having ceremonies done for you. There are free and inexpensive methods you can practice yourself. From Robert Svoboda I learned that there are patterns and activities that can perfectly align with each Energy System to help the system regain balance. As I continued my research, I began to recommend "remedies" to friends and colleagues and collected stories of results.

➤ My first conversation about remedies was with my friend, Jim. I explained that giving sweet-smelling flowers to young women every Friday can improve one's love life. (There are many alternate activities that will also work.) Jim was stunned. He told me that, in the one period of his life when he was happily in love, he regularly took flowers to the secretaries in his office (all young women) every Friday.

~~~

➢ My friend Caroline related her problems with her father and his new wife. The new wife categorically did not allow Caroline and her father to speak to each other. Caroline also worried about her daughter, who was in a precarious relationship and in tight financial circumstances. It turned out the same Energy System was involved in both situations. After doing the exercises for several weeks, Caroline was astonished. First, her father actually called her, and finally Caroline was able to call him without the new wife taking away the phone. Next, her daughter kicked out the deadbeat boyfriend and took steps to become financially responsible. We were both thrilled.

~~~

➢ Next was a family crisis. My developmentally disabled brother's spouse had become seriously dangerous. Suffering from a mental illness, she was attempting to buy a gun to kill our mother and hers, and threatened my brother if he told anyone. She had already drained his bank account, maxed out his credit cards, and coerced him into refinancing their condo. My brother was incapable of handling the complexities and danger of this situation.

Usually, balancing energies for others without their permission is hazardous, except in cases like this, where lives are at risk. This required all the efforts I could make. First, I consulted Ben Collins of _www.Puja.net_ to arrange energy-balancing ceremonies. He talked with temple priests to be sure our request was permissible, then arranged a series of ceremonies in several locations. I also did balancing activities of my own. Within two weeks, my brother's wife took the car and disappeared. This emboldened him to tell our mother the full situation and ask for a "rescue." Mom and I helped move him into in a safe-house near his work while we helped him pursue a divorce. Mom stayed with him and I continued my remedies from home.

Later, while in court, the wife extravagantly cursed her attorney who then quit. She failed to appear at the next hearing, relinquishing the few options she had left. We later learned she moved 2500 miles away. She never came back. My mother still shakes her head in amazement at how quickly a dangerous situation changed after we balanced the energies. (Years later, his sad ex-wife died of natural causes. I use her story knowing she has no surviving family members who would be embarrassed by it.)

~~~

➢ Lucy called me in tears. She was a successful realtor, accustomed to six figure annual incomes. When the market dropped, so did her business. Now, deep in a financial hole, Lucy had earned only $11,000 in the past fifteen months. She survived, panicking, by living with friends. Yet, only days after activating her remedies, she sold a three million dollar home, dramatically increasing her income.

~~~

➢ Matt, laid off from a high-performance corporate position a year earlier, was desperate. This was his third downsize in three years. Matt asked what could help him get back to work. The faulty Energy System was obvious. It was also responsible for his excruciating headaches. A week after he started his remedy activities, a top company that had previously strung him along for months finally offered him a good position. Matt continued the activities and noticed the headaches disappear as he became secure in his new position.

~~~

> Jeanne told me of her infant granddaughter's health problems. The child had already been hospitalized five times in her four brief months of life. The doctors couldn't figure out why she wasn't staying healthy. The child's chart pointed clearly to the dangerous Energy Systems, so we designed activities for the grandmother to perform on her behalf. Just days later, the child's health improved and, after this, the infections and hospitalizations did not recur.

~~~

This was exciting! At this juncture, I began looking ahead to anticipate signatures of changing energy systems. Perhaps we could stave off problems before they became severe.

~~~

> Rachel came to me in October with some general questions about her life. Immediately I saw a pattern that suggested grave danger to her daughter during a ten-day period the next March. It looked like her daughter would be involved in a life-threatening accident.

Rachel explained that her daughter would attend her first Iditarod (the famous dog-sled races) in Alaska during those days. Rachel immediately started doing activities that would protect her child. (Note: It was Rachel's pattern that indicated danger to her daughter, so we remediated Rachel's pattern, not the daughter's pattern.)

When the Iditarod was half over, Rachel received a phone call from her daughter. "You won't believe what just happened to me, Mom," the young woman said, "No one here can believe it either."

She was on the beginner's course and someone behind her lost control of dogs and sled. Dogs, sleds, and drivers ran over the daughter's sled, tangling with her dogs. Rachel's daughter was run over and dragged dozens of yards by multiple sleds and all the dogs. When everything stopped moving, the girl's face was less than an inch from the sled's "claw" – the fiercely toothed metal brake that clamps into ice to stop the sled. One more inch and her face would have been mangled, yet she walked away without a scratch on her body or a single broken bone. Her miraculous accident was the talk of the tournament.

~~~

➢ Later, in a routine analysis for Beverly, I saw a period of fire danger to her home. We identified the activities that would balance the energy and she began them. After the dangerous period passed, Beverly called to check in. She reported there was, indeed, a fire in her home at the expected time, but it was a small kitchen fire and easily contained.

~~~

➢ Then there was Jason, a man who was about to enter what looked like an extremely difficult period in his life. It suggested issues like bankruptcy and life-threatening illness. Before I frightened him with this news, I realized it was the mirror image of a period during his childhood, which he obviously survived. I asked him what happened at that point in his childhood. He said,

> Funny you should ask that. Those were weird years. All my friends were playing baseball and running around, and for some reason I became

obsessed with this old lady who lived by herself in a huge old mansion. She never left the house, and the kids mostly thought it was haunted. This old lady and I became friends, and I spent every single Saturday with her. Everyone thought I was nuts, and I really couldn't explain it.

I looked at him with my jaw hanging open and replied,

Those were EXACTLY the activities that could protect you during that time — and will protect you during the time ahead if you take similar actions, including doing them on Saturday! Either befriend a lonely and isolated old lady again — or better yet, continue to follow your already excellent instincts, and you'll be fine during this time.

~~~

These results inspired me to increase my research. I put together worksheets and started teaching people how to match their own issues to the twelve Energy Systems. I demonstrated how they could figure out for themselves which activities would change difficult patterns in their lives. I became aware of how a few individuals instinctively know what activities will balance their energies, despite having no conscious knowledge of the system. Now I'm putting this information into a book so that people I haven't met can use the techniques.

➢ Recently, I attended a concert with a friend. Sally told me that she used my worksheet handouts on balancing Energy Systems, and actually credited them with saving her life. She suffered from a painful, debilitating, and undiagnosed medical condition, and barely had the energy to eat and dress herself. With no relief in sight, she wondered why she was even alive. Between the pain, loss of energy, and lack of medical clarity she was losing hope. Sally told me that committing herself to the activities gave her a reason to keep going, and more importantly, it gave her hope during her most hopeless time. Simply taking action on her own behalf was meaningful and empowering. Before she completed the series of activities, her doctors finally began to unravel the medical mystery and her health situation dramatically improved.

~~~

You probably know this prayer, attributed to Reinhold Niebuhr, which speaks to what we can learn when we balance energy patterns:

SERENITY PRAYER

God grant me the serenity
to accept the things I cannot change,
courage to change the things I can,
and wisdom to know the difference.

The activities that follow help us realize this kind of wisdom. We are granted the patience and trust necessary to live well under difficult circumstances, whether or not they change. At the same time we get to change our own energetic environment so improvements become possible.

Use these activities. The cost in time and money is extremely low. The life-changing benefits are vast. The best you can get is a total change of the situation. The worst you can get is peace of mind. That's not bad.

~~~

As I was writing this section, a family situation arose that called for emergency energy balancing. My brother and his wife, after several miscarriages, had their first child way too early. The infant was born at twenty-two weeks' gestation, weighing barely over one pound. Only one child that premature is known to have survived, ever. I asked for and received my brother's permission to perform ceremonies for his son, and immediately emailed Ben Collins of the nonprofit group, _www.puja.net._ Ben was able to arrange a series of _pujas_ starting within twenty minutes of my call.

I know these were not the only efforts on my nephew's behalf. In addition to the skilled medical staff, many people were praying for him. Even so, his chance of surviving the first few days was minimal. He had no epidermis to protect him from dehydration and airborne germs. He had no solid bones. His eyes even lacked the slit that allows them to open. Babies born that early are usually miscarriages.

So far, my nephew has survived the many medical crises and appears to be alert and thriving. He has already lived three months — still 6 weeks short of his due date.

I can't say this infant's survival was due to the balancing ceremonies performed for him. I do know I felt a dramatic energy shift within hours of calling Ben. Sensing and observing such energy shifts is the reason I have been working with this system for the past twenty years. It's why I turn to the Vedic system of energy balancing when I'm in a pinch. And it's why I'm offering this book to you now. Even in the direst circumstances, these activities make life feel better.

ॐ

3. HOW DOES THIS WORK?

The bottom line is we don't know what these Energy Systems really are, or how the archetypally matched activities can possibly affect our lives. We can, however, offer some educated guesses as to what's happening:

> ➢ Any activity that gives us hope can make a difficult situation feel better.

> ➢ In situations where we feel powerless, the idea that we can actually do something to help reduces our sense of futility. This empowers us on an emotional level.

> ➢ When we perform these activities, we remind ourselves to imagine the positive outcome. This focus causes us to seek examples of positive results, which makes it more likely we will find them.

> ➢ When we think about balancing activities, we are NOT focused on the difficulties. Instead, we're distracted from negative thinking, which obviously makes us feel better.

> ➤ It is often said that our thoughts create our realities. If this is true, our focus on a positive outcome may actually help make it happen. What you focus on is what you get.

Those explanations appeal to the habits of modern western thinkers who prefer to say there is nothing magical here. It's a school of thought that dismisses unexplained effectiveness with the claim that we've simply created "self-fulfilling-prophecies." (In fact, self-fulfilling-prophecies are both unexplained and amazing.) This approach denies the possibility that something can happen that we don't understand or haven't "defined".

My experience shows that there is more going on than meets the eye. If ANY sincere effort would help, it wouldn't matter which energies you balanced. Yet, what we see is that _specific kinds of activities help specific kinds of situations_. The activity that restored the relationship between Beverly and her father could not protect Rachel's daughter, and neither of those activities could protect the health of Jeanne's grand-daughter. Only activities that relate to the off-balance Energy System can improve that system. The bond between the archetypal remedy activities and the specific Energy Systems is evidence that these systems are real, whether we see and understand these systems or not. Just because we don't yet understand something doesn't mean it doesn't exist.

The Energy Systems described in this handbook are not the only phenomena western science fails to understand. Gravity is a powerful example of a force science still struggles to explain. Nonetheless, no one denies it works. Medical cures often defy explanation. Here too, hundreds of years of experience show that they work.

Neither scientists nor astrologers can explain how and why astrology works; yet, clear historical evidence offers thousands of examples of how Energy Systems represented by the Sun, Moon and other planets shape our lives on earth. Richard Tarnas, a noted academic historian and astrologer, wrote a brilliant book, **_Cosmos and Psyche_** (see Bibliography). In it he examines the Energy Systems of planets over the course of recorded history. He demonstrates how these patterns are repeatedly and predictably associated with specific types of world events in politics, science, religion, the arts, and other aspects of human life.

THE SHOPPING CART ANALOGY

There may not be a scientific answer for how the balancing activities in this handbook work — at least not one that western analytical minds can easily grasp. Nevertheless, here's an analogy that seems useful for illustrating the big picture.

If you've ever been to a supermarket and grabbed a shopping cart with a damaged or unaligned wheel, you'll know how difficult it is to fight the imbalance. You spend so much energy avoiding crashes into shelving and other shoppers that you forget half your shopping list. If someone could wave a magic wand over that wheel so it would roll smoothly, the whole experience would be better. It's definitely worth the effort to go back and get a balanced shopping cart.

That's what these balancing energies can do in your life. Having off-balance Energy Systems causes us to waste our energy just trying to stay on track. We end up diverted from our life goals. Balancing them gives us a smooth experience with the "shopping cart" of life.

SYMBOLS AND ARCHETYPES

When we're working with Energy Systems, we're working with powerful and living archetypes. Carl Jung identified how the power of archetypal patterns shapes lives, events, and dreams even in the lives of people who, in their conscious minds, know nothing about archetypes. His patients' dreams would reveal elements of ancient mythologies, unknown to the dreamer, which paralleled and offered deeper insights into the dreamer's concerns. Once Jung realized that astrological planetary energies embodied the same ancient archetypes (and unknown to most people), he used astrological analysis to work with each of his clients. Jung's daughter undertook the arduous task of learning the mathematics of astrology long before computers were available for the task. She provided Jung with the archetypal/astrological data patterns that applied to his clients before he met them. Jung was using "Energy Systems."

Once you enter the realm of symbols, you enter a world without sharp definition, and with many rich associations. The world of archetypes is a world of symbols. You can comprehend how broad a symbol can be and also how clearly exclusive it can be if you imagine a symbol for *Happiness*. An interpretation of that imagined symbol could include thousands of events, ideas, circumstances, and words. Though the thousands of symbols seem infinite, they have clear boundaries. Categorically excluded from the world of *"Happiness"* would be the experience encompassed by the loss of a loved one (*"Sad"*). That has to be part of a totally different symbol. The archetype containing *"Happiness"* is a different archetype than the one containing *"Death of a loved one."*

If you illustrate Energy Systems in a Venn diagram (see figure), the overlapping circles show where the combined systems create specific and more detailed energy patterns. Using our imaginary *Happiness* symbol as an example, we overlap it with a *Busy* symbol and a *Resting* symbol to more precisely understand the kind of *Happiness* a person may experience. Planetary Energy Systems also overlap to give us more precise information about situations in people's lives.

The Vedas demonstrate a deep and abiding under-standing of these Energy Systems. They teach us how to identify which archetypes we engage, and how to invoke the

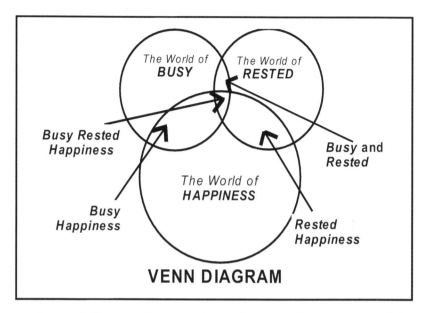

VENN DIAGRAM

archetypal Energy Systems in order to enhance or modify original patterns in our lives.

4. WHAT IS KARMA?
and
CAN WE CHANGE IT?

I'm often asked if balancing activities will always fix problems. The answer is No; yet they will always ameliorate the situation in some way. These activities work because they become part of your karma. To make this clear, let's examine the Vedic concepts of *karma*.

TYPES OF KARMA

The word *karma* has entered the English language; but if you ask a dozen people what it means, you'll get a dozen different answers. *Karma* is such a deep and complex concept that there are literally many different types according to the Vedas. The overall definition indicates cause and effect. The Bible expresses this with "*As you sow, so shall you reap.*" As we learn how to balance Energy Systems in our lives, it is useful to understand some different subsets of the larger concept of *karma.*

29

The Karma Pot

One type of *karma* we can compare to a great soup pot. I call it the *karma pot*. This pot stores all the *karma* we've accumulated from all our previous lifetimes and haven't yet used. In each incarnation, we scoop out a portion to experience. This great soup pot contains good *karma* and bad *karma*. It has nice pieces of potatoes and carrots and perhaps even pieces of meat. However, it also has onion-skins, tough ends of broccoli, gristle, stones, and other indigestible material. In each lifetime, all our actions, both good and bad, go into that "karma-pot" to sweeten or sour the "karmic soup" for future lifetimes.

Occasionally, people ask if their suffering now is because they were a terrible person in a former life. This conclusion is highly unlikely, and is also irrelevant. Each of us has done our share of wrong over our many incarnations. Each of us has also done much good. It can simply be chance that someone's lifetime ladle brought up all the undesirable parts of their *karma*-soup. Some souls deliberately choose the bad pieces for a particular lifetime in order to finish them and leave more good *karma* in the pot for the next time. A few advanced souls have the option of choosing a "coffee-break" life after eons of hard work.

Once we're born, however, the specific "portion of soup" for this life is set, and within this ladle of *karma* there are several more categories of *karma*.

Fixed Karma

Some karmic conditions are simply unchangeable. They are what they are and the best we can do is enjoy them if they're pleasant or learn to accept them if they are unpleasant. The good news is that difficult conditions become easier to tolerate when we work to balance the energies. Oddly enough, people like Bill Gates or Oprah Winfrey have large portions of their lives governed by fixed *karma* having to do with money and fame. These people couldn't be poor and unknown if they wanted to be!

If you ever saw an episode of **Fantasy Island** on TV you'll remember Herve Villechaize, the Little Person who greeted all guests to **Fantasy Island**. Herve had a karmic pattern for fame, but if he had wanted to be an NBA basketball star, Herve would have failed spectacularly. His stature alone would lead him to fail, and because he had fixed *karma* for fame, Herve's failure would have been front-page news.

One of my teachers had a client who was highly educated and lived in abject poverty. She wanted to know how to win the lottery using Vedic remedies. After a study of her Vedic astrological chart, he determined that fixed *karma* would deny her this financial windfall. She said,

> That can't be true. I don't believe we're "stuck" with anything. I believe we can always change our *karma* with application, effort and right thought!

He responded,

> And so do I. I'm just saying in *this* lifetime there isn't enough time for you to change enough patterns to win the lottery. There are too many poverty indicators and virtually no wealth indicators. This creates fixed *karma* for this lifetime. However, you can change your future lives and make your present more bearable by doing remedies now.

It is rare that a karmic pattern is so strong that it can't be changed. Even in those cases, balancing activities help. In my own case, the karmic pattern revealed by Vedic astrology indicated categorically and with no "wiggle-room" that I would not have children. After years of wanting them, trying,

31

and for various reasons not having them, it was really a relief to learn this. I was lucky. I could see the benefits and could stop worrying. Not having children allowed me a career I loved—one that was financially inadequate to support a family. I suspect my reaction was benign because of the balancing activities I practiced for so long.

When you face unwanted fixed *karma,* balancing Energy Systems will definitely move your life in the right direction. You may begin to see the good side of the situation or you may discover that the *karma* wasn't all that "fixed" after all. If nothing else changes, the capacity to be at peace with life is still a very good outcome.

Stuck Karma

Another type of *karma* is an energy pattern that appears "stuck," although it CAN be changed with effort. A young man named Muggsy Bogues wanted to be a basketball star -- but he was only five feet, three inches tall. Competing against people who were almost two feet taller certainly didn't make his goal easy. Nevertheless, Bogues had a fourteen-year NBA career as a star athlete. His success is an example of a karmic pattern (too short to be an NBA star) that was overcome with extraordinary efforts.

Changeable Karma

In most cases, we only need a little nudge to move a situation in the desired direction. This is "changeable *karma,*" and requires relatively little effort to create the results we want. These situations respond quickly to balancing activities. Since this applies to most situations, it is a good argument for always trying the remedies!

Free Will

Anything not covered by FIXED, STUCK, or CHANGEABLE KARMA falls in the category of utter free will. There's an irony here: If there isn't enough unbalanced energy to make you strongly desire something, you probably won't persevere long enough to create new patterns. This leads us to the odd but logical conclusion that our only free will is in efforts to change STUCK or CHANGEABLE KARMAS. If we're destined to be rich and famous, we can't change it. If there are no indications at all, we probably don't care. It is only when we are challenged that we can exercise free will. Oprah's and Bill Gates' free will is in how they use their fame and wealth. Their fixed *karma* gives them no option for poverty and obscurity.

HELPING OTHERS

Once we learn how powerful these practices are, it is tempting to apply them to friends and family members to improve their lives, too. Yet, doing so quickly becomes a very sticky situation.

If you are the parent of a minor, or if you have legal guardianship over someone, you can perform activities on their behalf without negative consequence. Alternatively, if you see a person in an immediate life-threatening situation, most certainly you can help. Here are the conditions under which you CANNOT safely help others:

- You CANNOT help a child
  - who is NOT your own child;
  - who is over eighteen years old (even if it is your own child);
  - who is legally independent of you;
  - if you don't have the authority of legal guardianship,

➢ unless that child is in immediate peril (including living with physically abusive parents/guardians).

🔸 You cannot help an adult

➢ unless that person is in immediate danger of dying from his or her actions or inactions;

➢ Unless you have legal guardianship over that person.

You can get yourself and your loved ones into a real karmic mess when you rush in to help. You may think you're being thoughtful, yet some "help" may cause great damage.

There is an old story about a man watching a butterfly emerge from a cocoon. It was a slow process, and his sympathies were with the small creature as it struggled to emerge from a tiny hole in its chrysalis. Finally, the man decided to help. Very carefully, he took cuticle scissors and lengthened the hole where the butterfly was struggling. This appeared to work, because very soon the butterfly came out — but its wings were all crumpled. The man waited, hoping they would straighten out with time, but they did not. The wings dried and hardened, still crumpled.

At last, the man checked with experts who told him the butterfly's struggle to emerge was what stretched and straightened its wings. Without the struggle, the wings weren't pressed into usefulness. His butterfly would never fly. Similarly, we can cripple other people when we jump in too eagerly to help.

My teachers stressed to me the importance of "non-interference." They taught that to step in and "fix" the life experience of another independent adult is to interfere with both free will and the learning processes of the other person. If we see others who need help, we can offer to help, yet we can neither force them nor do it for them. They must take action for themselves.

My grandmother was a master at not forcing her help on people, yet she was beloved as a wise and helpful person. She watched me struggle with typical teenager situations — messes with boyfriends, or tussles within a clique of girls -- and she would say, "I have some ideas about that if you'd like to hear them." Then she'd shut up. It wouldn't take long for my curiosity to overcome teen-aged independence and I'd ask her. I knew I was free to follow her suggestions or ignore them. Without any pressure, I usually felt free to adopt her approach. It was my choice to ask for her help. She simply let me know it was available.

We have often been told how valuable life on earth is. What we can learn in one lifetime might take eons without physical bodies. If you remove the difficulties from another adult's life without her permission, you deny her the learning potential of this rare and valuable lifetime. What's more, you will take on the karma of stunting her growth. You can (and should) always offer help, but if your offer isn't accepted, don't interfere.

This does not mean there is no way to help others from a distance. As you learn more about each Energy System, you will discover that there are some systems that include your father, one that includes your mother, and other systems for relatives, spouses, friends, children, *etc.*

If YOU, in YOUR LIFE, are suffering because of the difficulties of your spouse, for example, you can balance the Energy System in YOUR LIFE that represents "spouse." If your spouse has a heart condition, balance "spouse", rather than "heart condition." If your mother can't handle her finances and this upsets you, balance energies for "mother" but not for "finances."

You can balance Energy Systems that represent those people in your life whose well-being affects your own. What you CANNOT DO is address the particular ISSUE you see as the problem. The activities you do are for YOU. Surprisingly, this approach often brings us the results we really wanted.

If you wish to help individuals in a more direct way, you can ask these people if they would allow you to have ceremonies performed to help with the specific issue. If they are uncomfortable with cultures different from their own, you can substitute ceremonies from their own culture or religion that partake of the same Energy System archetypes. If you do not have permission to help, you can arrange ceremonies for YOURSELF, to balance the Energy System relating to "mother," or "spouse," or whatever energy group applies to that person's place in your life.

PART II:

Assessment

Illustration 3

Souls Rise and Fall

SILK TAPESTRY BY ANNE BEVERSDORF
Based on a vision of HILDEGARD VON BINGEN.

In Hildegard's vision, souls are imagined as stars,
some rising from the dark lower world to the heavens,
and some falling from heaven to the earth below.

Color image may be viewed at:
http://www.sacred-threads.com/tapestries-2/hildegard-von-bingen-inspired/souls-rise-and-fall/

"Souls Rise and Fall"

5. ASSESSING YOUR ENERGY PATTERNS

Twelve distinct Energy Systems must be balanced for our lives to run smoothly. For most of us, one or more of these systems is out of balance. In the pages that follow, you will find assessment sheets you can use to determine which ESs need balancing to make your life better. (For convenience, I'm using the abbreviation ES to represent Energy System.)

If ANY of the words or phrases in these lists represents such a huge factor in your life that it colors all else (for instance, under ES2/Moon is the word "diabetes," a disease which could easily compromise your quality of life), feel free to make up your own rating for that item. In other words, if you have such severe diabetes that you are unable to hold a job or carry on normal activities, feel free to assign as many as 100 extra points next to the word "diabetes." Alternatively, if "depression" overwhelms you, feel free to give that single word as many points as you wish. In fact, if you have a big problem represented by any word or phrase on these lists it means you should immediately balance energies for that system. You can even go directly to *Appendix C: Matching Problems to Remedies* or to the index of this book to see if that word is specifically listed. Don't worry if it isn't, though. The themes in the questionnaire will pick up the pattern.

The rating system is included because many people feel more comfortable if they can objectify and rank their subjective experiences. Other people would rather simply scan the lists and see if they recognize anything. For them assessments and ratings may be intimidating or irrelevant.

If, for any reason, you would rather not complete the ratings and calculations, your subjective analysis of each Energy System is a reliable indicator for your balancing needs. Simply read through the qualities and problems listed under each ES and make a few notes for yourself when you recognize a group of your issues under a single Energy System. Then proceed to the Balancing Energies pages for the ES you've identified as important to you.

6. ASSESSMENT SHEETS

For each of the twelve energies, you will see the headings **GOOD QUALITIES** and **PROBLEMS**, with words and sentences listed underneath. You have the opportunity to improve things in your life:

➤ if your quality of life suffers because you <u>lack the good qualities,</u> or

➤ if your quality of life suffers because you <u>have too many of the problems</u> listed.

Use a scale of zero to five to rank each of the qualities or problems.

➤ A ranking of <u>ZERO</u> means this is <u>not</u> an issue for you.

➤ A ranking of <u>FIVE</u> mean this issue needs to change.

For example, under the heading **<u>GOOD QUALITIES</u>**,

➢ a <u>ZERO</u> ranking next to a word or sentence means you suffer no problems because you lack this quality. You may have the quality in abundance, or maybe it simply is not an issue for you. You don't need more.

➢ a ranking of <u>FIVE</u> means you need a whole lot more of this quality for your life to be better.

Under the heading **<u>PROBLEMS</u>**,

➢ a <u>ZERO</u> ranking means this is not a problem for you, or the problem is irrelevant to your happiness.

➢ a ranking of <u>FIVE</u> means this is a significant problem for you, and your life would be much better if this issue improved.

ASSESSMENT: ENERGY SYSTEM 1/SUN

ES1/Sun 1 -- 1A: <u>GOOD QUALITIES</u>.

Score on a scale of 0 to 5.

Think about how these qualities affect your happiness. Then finish the sentences under the RATING GUIDE.

- <u>Zero</u> means you <u>have enough</u> of this quality. You do NOT need more for your life to function well.
- <u>Three</u> means you don't need much but you aren't suffering much from a lack.
- <u>Five</u> means you <u>need more</u> of this quality for your life to function well.

RATING GUIDE					
0	1	2	3	4	5
|------------|---------------|---------------|---------------|--------------|					
I have enough...		Maybe I need a little more...		I need more...	

<u>Rating</u> | <u>Quality</u>

_____* <u>ambition</u> to make my life work well.

_____* natural <u>authority</u> for my life to work well.

_____* <u>boldness</u> for my life to work well.

_____* <u>charisma</u> to make my life work well.

_____* <u>consciousness</u> about my own motivations, and of the people and events around me.

_____* <u>creativity</u> for my life to work well.

_____* <u>dignity</u> in the way I conduct myself to make things work well for me.

_____* <u>energy</u> for life to work well for me.

45

_____* <u>faith</u> in the goodness of life.

_____* <u>fame</u> for my life to work well.

_____* <u>generosity</u> toward others for my life to work well.

_____* ease in <u>giving orders</u> and <u>directing others.</u>

_____* <u>grace</u> in my body, or in the way I handle sticky situations for my life to work well.

_____* <u>happiness</u> to function well.

_____* <u>hopefulness</u> about life in general.

_____* <u>individualism</u> to help me in life.

_____* skill in <u>influencing</u> people and situations.

_____* <u>leadership</u> abilities for my life to work well.

_____* <u>loyalty</u> to others to make my life good.

_____* <u>nobility</u> in my attitudes or actions to make my life successful.

_____* <u>optimism</u> for my life to be happy and successful.

_____* <u>power</u> over myself, situations, and events to be happy and successful.

_____* <u>regard</u> for the welfare of others.

_____* good <u>reputation</u> in the world around me to make my life successful and happy.

_____* <u>respect for elders</u> so my life can be successful and happy.

_____* <u>status</u> for my life's happiness and functionality.

_____* <u>steadiness</u> and stability for my life to be successful and happy.

_____* <u>vitality</u> for my life to be successful and happy.

_____* <u>worldly success</u> to satisfy me.

_____**SUBTOTAL 1-A**

~~~

ES1/Sun -- 1-B: **PROBLEMS.** Score on a scale of 0 to 5.

Think about how these issues affect your happiness. Then finish the sentences under the RATING GUIDE.

- <u>Zero</u> means you <u>have no problems with this issue</u>. You do NOT need help for your life to function well.
- <u>Three</u> means you may have some difficulties but you aren't suffering greatly from them.
- <u>Five</u> means you <u>need to resolve this issue</u> for your life to function well.

RATING GUIDE

0	1	2	3	4	5

| ------------- | --------------- | --------------- | --------------- | --------------- | ------------- |

I have no problems with...   I have some problems with...

I have big problems with...

<u>Rating</u> | <u>Problems</u>

_____* <u>altercations</u> with authorities.

_____* being too <u>ambitious,</u> or others saying I'm too ambitious.

_____* <u>back trouble</u>.

_____* being too <u>bossy,</u> or others telling me I'm too bossy.

_____* others complaining that I <u>brag</u> too much.

_____* people complaining that I need to be the <u>center of attention.</u>

_____* the health of my <u>eyes</u> or my <u>vision</u>.

_____* managing issues with my <u>father</u>.

_____* <u>government harassment</u>.

48

_____* heart disease.

_____* thinking I need to be in charge of everything.

_____* jealousy--I am too jealous or others are jealous of me.

_____* people telling me I'm selfish.

_____* people thinking I'm showing off.

_____* skin diseases.

_____* people thinking I'm stuck up.

_____* people thinking I'm too full of myself.

_____* others thinking I don't treat other people or animals well.

_____* not trusting that everything will turn out for the best.

_____**SUBTOTAL 1-B**

~~~

TOTAL: _____ (Add subtotals A plus B)

SCORING: Multiply total by 1.20 for Score 1. (*e.g.,* if your total is 80, the score will be 80 + 20% of 80--which is 16. So 80 plus 16 = 96.)

<div align="center">

TOTAL:_____

X___**1.20**

SCORE =_____

ES1/Sun: **RECORD SCORE 1 HERE:**_____

Copy this score to page 99.

</div>

ASSESSMENT: ENERGY SYSTEM 2/MOON

ES2/Moon – 2-A: <u>GOOD QUALITIES</u>.

Score on a scale of 0 to 5.

> Think about how these qualities affect your happiness. Then finish the sentences under the RATING GUIDE.
> - <u>Zero</u> means you <u>have enough</u> of this quality. You do NOT need more for your life to function well.
> - <u>Three</u> means you don't need much but you aren't suffering much from a lack.
> - <u>Five</u> means you <u>need more</u> of this quality for your life to function well.

RATING GUIDE					
0	1	2	3	4	5
|------------|---------------|--------------|---------------|---------------|					
I have enough...		Maybe I need a little more...		I need more...	

<u>Rating</u>|<u>Quality</u>

_____* <u>emotional stability</u> for my life to function well.

_____* <u>good, stable habits</u> for my life to function well.

_____* <u>imagination</u> for my life to work better.

_____* ability to <u>nurture</u> myself and others for life to be better.

_____* ability to <u>receive</u> insights and impressions from the world around me.

_____* ability to <u>remember</u> things reliably.

_____<u>SUBTOTAL 2-A</u>

~~~

ES2/Moon -- 2-B: **PROBLEMS**.

Score on a scale of 0 to 5.

> Think about how these issues affect your happiness. Then finish the sentences under the RATING GUIDE.
> - Zero means you <u>have no problems with this issue</u>. You do NOT need help for your life to function well.
> - Three means you may have some difficulties but you aren't suffering greatly from them.
> - Five means you <u>need to resolve this issue</u> for your life to function well.

RATING GUIDE					
0	1	2	3	4	5

```
|--------------|--------------|--------------|--------------|--------------|
I have no problems with...      I have some problems with...
                                    I have big problems with...
```

<u>Rating</u> | <u>Problem</u>

_____* <u>anxiety</u> that interferes with my functioning well in life.

_____* <u>asthma</u> that interferes with my functioning well in life.

_____* <u>blood diseases</u> that interfere with my functioning well in life.

_____* <u>bronchitis</u> that interferes with my good life.

_____* <u>coughs</u> that interfere with my good life.

_____* vulnerability to <u>temptation</u> that interferes with my life goals.

_____* <u>emotional upheavals</u> that interrupt my life.

_____* <u>eye diseases</u> that make my life difficult.

_____* getting in touch with my <u>feelings</u>, and this problem creates hardships in my life.

_____* being <u>fickle</u> or <u>changing my mind</u> too often, in a way that seriously disrupts my life.

_____* being <u>hypersensitive</u> to others' words, actions or inactions, such that it causes more problems for me.

_____* being <u>indecisive</u> in ways that disrupt my life.

_____* <u>intestinal disorders</u>.

_____* managing situations with my <u>mother</u>.

_____* <u>over-reacting</u> to situations or people that causes difficulties in my life.

_____* <u>paralysis</u> (physical or emotional).

_____* loss of <u>sense of taste or smell</u>.

_____* <u>stomach problems</u> that disrupt my life.

_____* <u>swellings</u> in my body.

_____* <u>throat</u> problems, like frequent sore throats, choking, difficulty swallowing.

_____* <u>thyroid problems</u>.

_____* <u>tumors</u>.

_____* <u>varicose veins</u>.

_____* <u>water retention</u>.

_____**SUBTOTAL 2-B**

TOTAL:_____ (Add subtotals A plus B)

SCORING: Multiply total by 2 for Score 2.

TOTAL:_____

X____2

SCORE =_____

ES2/Moon: **RECORD SCORE 2 HERE:**_____

Copy this score to page 99.

ASSESSMENT: ENERGY SYSTEM 3/MARS

ES3/Mars -- 3-A: **GOOD QUALITIES**.
Score on a scale of 0 to 5.

Think about how these qualities affect your happiness. Then finish the sentences under the RATING GUIDE.
- <u>Zero</u> means you <u>have enough</u> of this quality. You do NOT need more for your life to function well.
- <u>Three</u> means you don't need much but you aren't suffering much from a lack.
- <u>Five</u> means you <u>need more</u> of this quality for your life to function well.

RATING GUIDE					
0	1	2	3	4	5

| -------------- | --------------- | -------------- | --------------- | --------------- | |

I have enough...   Maybe I need a little more...   I need more...

Rating | Quality

_____* eagerness to take <u>action</u> for my life to function well.

_____* <u>ambition</u> for my life to function well.

_____* <u>competitive spirit</u> for my life to function well.

_____* <u>courage</u> to succeed when I need to.

_____* <u>endurance</u> to complete what I must do.

_____* <u>energy</u> to do what I want to in life.

_____* <u>force of character</u> for others to respect me, so that my life functions well.

_____* <u>goal-directed energy</u> to accomplish what I wish in life.

_____* <u>muscular strength</u> to support my choices in life.

54

_____* <u>passion</u> to accomplish what I want to do.

_____* <u>self-confidence</u> to do what I need.

_____* <u>strength</u> (both physical and strength of character) to accomplish what I wish.

_____* <u>vigor</u> to engage in the activities I desire.

_____* <u>sharp wit</u> to support my life's goals.

_____**SUBTOTAL 3-A**

~ ~ ~

ES3/Mars -- 3-B: **PROBLEMS**. Score on a scale of 0 to 5.

Think about how these issues affect your happiness. Then finish the sentences under the RATING GUIDE.

- <u>Zero</u> means you <u>have no problems with this issue</u>. You do NOT need help for your life to function well.
- <u>Three</u> means you may have some difficulties but you aren't suffering greatly from them.
- <u>Five</u> means you <u>need to resolve this issue</u> for your life to function well.

RATING GUIDE					
0	1	2	3	4	5

|--------------|---------------|--------------|---------------|--------------|--------------|

I have no problems with...   I have some problems with...

I have big problems with...

Rating | Problem

_____* people telling me I'm <u>abrupt</u> (curt, impatient) in dealings with others, or other people are frequently abrupt with me.

_____* being <u>accident-prone</u>.

_____* getting into or handling <u>adversarial situations</u> that diminish my quality of life.

_____* people complaining I have an <u>"all-or-nothing"</u> attitude, or dealing with others with this attitude.

_____* <u>anger management</u>, or others becoming <u>angry</u> with me.

_____* <u>appendicitis</u>.

_____* people complaining that I'm <u>argumentative</u> or I get into arguments that complicate my life.

_____* getting <u>burned</u>, more than most people.

_____* <u>changing my mind</u> frequently, such that it interferes with my success.

_____* getting into <u>conflicts with others</u> that diminish my quality of life.

_____* lacking <u>courage</u> to pursue what I want.

_____* too many <u>cuts and scrapes</u>.

_____* having frequent <u>fevers</u>.

_____* <u>hemorrhages</u>.

_____* being <u>impatient</u>, so that it reduces my quality of life.

_____* <u>inflammatory illnesses</u>.

_____* with physical <u>injuries</u> often enough or bad enough that they reduce my effectiveness in life.

_____* too easily getting <u>irritated</u> with others, or others are frequently irritated with me.

_____* frequently thinking, <u>"I shouldn't have done that!"</u>

_____* <u>jumping into things</u> too quickly.

_____* getting so frustrated when others make errors that I want to <u>lash out</u> (or others lash out at me when I make errors).

_____* <u>legal problems</u>.

_____* <u>multiple surgeries</u> that interfere with my life goals.

_____* lacking enough <u>stamina</u> to pursue what I want.

_____* being so <u>obsessive</u> about some things that it reduces my quality of life.

_____* frequent <u>rashes</u>.

_____* managing issues with my <u>siblings</u>.

_____* being unable to <u>stick to</u> things, so that it interferes with accomplishments.

_____* <u>ulcers</u>.

_____* being a <u>victim of violence</u>.

_____* getting so angry I want to do something <u>violent.</u>

_____**SUBTOTAL 3-B**

~~~

TOTAL:_____ (Sum of subtotals A plus B)

SCORING: Multiply total by 1.25 for Score 3 (*e.g.*, if your score is 80, add 80 to 25% of 80 for a score of 100).

TOTAL:_____

X   1.25

SCORE =_____

ES3/Mars: **RECORD SCORE 3 HERE:**_____

Copy this score to page 99.

ASSESSMENT: ENERGY SYSTEM 4/MERCURY

ES4/Mercury -- 4-A: **GOOD QUALITIES**.

Score on a scale of 0 to 5.

> Think about how these qualities affect your happiness. Then finish the sentences under the RATING GUIDE.
> - Zero means you <u>have enough</u> of this quality. You do NOT need more for your life to function well.
> - <u>Three</u> means you don't need much but you aren't suffering much from a lack.
> - <u>Five</u> means you <u>need more</u> of this quality for your life to function well.

RATING GUIDE
0   1   2   3   4   5
|-------------|---------------|---------------|---------------|---------------|
I have enough...   Maybe I need a little more...   I need more...

Rating | Quality

_____* <u>analytical skill</u> for my life to be successful.

_____* <u>calculating cleverness</u> to smooth my way in life.

_____* <u>communication skills</u> to succeed.

_____* <u>craftsmanship</u> ability for my life to function well.

_____* <u>detail orientation</u> to help my life function smoothly.

_____* physical or mental <u>dexterity</u> to succeed.

_____* <u>diplomatic skill</u> to succeed.

_____* <u>handyman skill</u> to be happy with my life.

_____* <u>intelligence</u> to succeed at what I want.

_____* <u>marketing skills</u> to succeed at what I want.

_____* <u>mental discrimination</u> to succeed in life.

_____* ability to be <u>rational</u> about situations.

_____* all-purpose <u>skillfulness</u> to succeed.

_____* <u>speaking ability</u> to succeed.

_____* <u>study skills</u> to succeed.

_____* <u>verbal ability</u> to succeed in life.

_____* quick <u>wit</u> to make my life happy.

_____* <u>writing skill</u> to make my life run smoothly.

_____**SUBTOTAL 4-A**

~~~

ES4/Mercury -- 4-B: **PROBLEMS**.

Score on a scale of 0 to 5.

> Think about how these issues affect your happiness. Then finish the sentences under the RATING GUIDE.
> - <u>Zero</u> means you <u>have no problems with this issue</u>. You do NOT need help for your life to function well.
> - <u>Three</u> means you may have some difficulties but you aren't suffering greatly from them.
> - <u>Five</u> means you <u>need to resolve this issue</u> for your life to function well.

RATING GUIDE					
0	1	2	3	4	5

|---------------|---------------|---------------|---------------|---------------|

I have no problems with...   I have some problems with...

I have big problems with...

<u>Rating</u> | <u>Problem</u>

_____* being too <u>aloof</u> or "stand-offish."

_____* <u>brain diseases</u>.

_____* being <u>deceived</u> by others, or by situations.

_____* difficulties <u>communicating</u> clearly or on time, so that it reduces my effectiveness.

_____* making <u>decisions</u>, such that it interferes with my life.

_____* <u>gout</u>.

_____* an <u>inability to study</u>.

_____* lack of <u>mental sharpness</u> such that it reduces my quality of life.

_____* lethargy, such that it interferes with my life.

_____* lung diseases.

_____* memory lapses.

_____* mental depression.

_____* consequences resulting from misleading others.

_____* nervousness, such that it reduces my effectiveness in life.

_____* over-thinking things, or being so "in my head" about things that my effectiveness is reduced.

_____* having received a poor education.

_____* consequences of not caring much about "right and wrong."

_____* the consequences of stealing or being a target of thieves.

_____* stuttering or stammering.

_____* vertigo (dizziness).

_____**SUBTOTAL 4-B**

~~~

TOTAL:_____ (Sum of subtotals A plus B)

SCORING: Multiply total by 2 for Score 4.

TOTAL:_____

X____2

SCORE = _____

ES4/Mercury: **RECORD SCORE 4 HERE:**_____

Copy this score to page 99.

ASSESSMENT: ENERGY SYSTEM 5/JUPITER

ES5/Jupiter – 5-A: **GOOD QUALITIES**.

Score on a scale of 0 to 5.

Think about how these qualities affect your happiness. Then finish the sentences under the RATING GUIDE.

- **Zero** means you <u>have enough</u> of this quality. You do NOT need more for your life to function well.
- **Three** means you don't need much but you aren't suffering much from a lack.
- **Five** means you <u>need more</u> of this for your life to function well.

RATING GUIDE					
0	1	2	3	4	5
|-------------	---------------	---------------	---------------	---------------	-------------|
I am...		Maybe I should be a little more...		I should be more...	

<u>Rating</u> | <u>Quality</u>

_____* <u>buoyant</u>--able to bounce back after difficulties.

_____* <u>cheerful</u>.

_____* <u>easy-going</u>.

_____* well <u>educated</u>--enough to meet my life goals.

_____* <u>friendly</u>.

_____* <u>fruitful</u>, able to produce children, ideas, results.

_____* <u>generous</u>.

_____* <u>gentle</u>.

_____* comfortable with my <u>good judgment</u>.

_____* <u>growth-oriented</u>.

_____* <u>high-minded</u>.

_____* <u>hopeful</u>.

_____* <u>humanitarian</u>.

_____* <u>humorous</u>.

_____* <u>idealistic</u>.

_____* <u>inclusive</u> of other people and ideas.

_____* <u>kind-hearted</u>.

_____* <u>optimistic</u>.

_____* a person with a highly <u>spiritual outlook</u> on life.

_____* <u>sociable</u>.

_____* <u>soft-hearted</u>.

_____* full of <u>faith</u> in the goodness of life.

_____**SUBTOTAL 5-A**

~~~

ES5/Jupiter -- 5-B: **PROBLEMS**:

Score on a scale of 0 to 5.

> Think about how these issues affect your happiness. Then finish the sentences under the RATING GUIDE.
> - <u>Zero</u> means you <u>have no problems with this issue</u>. You do NOT need help for your life to function well.
> - <u>Three</u> means you may have some difficulties but you aren't suffering greatly from them.
> - <u>Five</u> means you <u>need to resolve this issue</u> for your life to function well.

> ### RATING GUIDE
>
> 0   1   2   3   4   5
>
> |--------------|---------------|---------------|--------------|---------------|
>
> I have no problems with...   I have some problems with...
>
>   I have big problems with...

<u>Rating</u> | <u>Problem</u>

_____* others complaining that I think I'm "<u>always right.</u>"

_____* others complaining that I'm <u>argumentative</u>.

_____* consequences of <u>bad judgment</u>.

_____* consequences from <u>bad speculations</u>, investments, or gambling.

_____* <u>carelessness</u> that reduces the quality of my life.

_____* conceiving or having <u>children</u>.

_____* the health and well-being of my <u>children</u>.

_____* <u>circulatory congestion</u>.

_____* <u>debts</u> or indebtedness.

_____* being easily <u>deceived</u>.

_____* <u>diabetes</u>.

_____* obtaining good <u>educational opportunities</u>.

_____* the quality of my <u>education</u>.

_____* consequences of <u>entertaining false hopes</u> about others, or about the future (overly optimistic).

_____* <u>extravagance</u>.

_____* others complaining that I'm <u>greedy</u> or <u>selfish</u>.

_____* <u>hearing</u> or the health of my ears.

_____* having <u>poor boundaries</u> in relation to others.

_____* <u>liver disease</u>.

_____* <u>lymphatic congestion</u>.

_____* consequences of not following the <u>moral values</u> of my community.

_____* <u>obesity</u>.

_____* being <u>overindulgent</u> with myself or others.

_____* consequences of <u>risqué</u> behavior.

_____* getting along with <u>teachers</u> or mentors.

_____* <u>too much generosity</u> which is reducing the quality of my life.

_____SUBTOTAL 5-B

TOTAL: _____ (Sum of subtotals A plus B)

SCORING: Multiply total by 1.20 for Score 5. (*E.g* if your total is 80, the score will be 80 + 20% of 80, or 96.)

TOTAL:_____

X__1.20

SCORE = _____

ES5/Jupiter: **RECORD SCORE 5 HERE:_____**

Copy score to page 99.

ASSESSMENT: ENERGY SYSTEM 6/VENUS

ES6/Venus -- 6-A: **GOOD QUALITIES**.
Score on a scale of 0 to 5.

Think about how these qualities affect your happiness. Then finish the sentences under the RATING GUIDE.

- <u>Zero</u> means you <u>have enough</u> of this quality. You do NOT need more for your life to function well.
- <u>Three</u> means you don't need much but you aren't suffering much from a lack.
- <u>Five</u> means you <u>need more</u> of this for your life to function well.

RATING GUIDE					
0	1	2	3	4	5
|-------------	|---------------	|---------------	|---------------	|---------------	|
I am...		Maybe I should be a little more...		I should be more...	

<u>Rating | Quality</u>

_____* <u>affectionate</u> to make my life more pleasing.

_____* <u>artistic</u> to be happy with life.

_____* <u>attractive</u> to make my life happy.

_____* <u>balanced</u> in my approach to others.

_____* a <u>creator of harmony</u> such that my life is pleasing to myself and others.

_____* <u>diplomatic</u> in order to succeed.

_____* <u>elegant</u> to give pleasure to myself and others.

_____* <u>friendly</u>.

_____* focused on <u>love</u>.

69

_____* <u>graceful</u> to please myself and others.

_____* <u>harmonious</u> in my attitude to situations and other people.

_____* <u>kind</u>.

_____* a <u>peacemaker</u>.

_____* <u>sensually refined</u> (appreciate things of quality — e.g. a *gourmet*, not a *gourmand, etc.*).

_____* <u>skilled at making beautiful things</u>.

_____* <u>sociable</u> for my ease and happiness.

_____**SUBTOTAL 6-A**

~~~

ES6/Venus -- 6-B: **PROBLEMS**:

Score on a scale of 0 to 5.

> Think about how these issues affect your happiness. Then finish the sentences under the RATING GUIDE.
> - <u>Zero</u> means you <u>have no problems with this issue</u>. You do NOT need help for your life to function well.
> - <u>Three</u> means you may have some difficulties but you aren't suffering greatly from them.
> - <u>Five</u> means you <u>need to resolve this issue</u> for your life to function well.

RATING GUIDE

```
0          1          2          3          4          5
|----------|----------|----------|----------|----------|
I have no problems with...    I have some problems with...
                                     I have big problems with...
```

<u>Rating</u> | <u>Problem</u>

_____* feeling <u>I deserve more</u> from other people.

_____* <u>diseases</u> of the <u>sexual organs</u> (not necessarily STDs).

_____* my <u>disinterest in taste or style</u>, causing people to judge me harshly.

_____* <u>gout</u>.

_____* <u>laziness</u> that catches up with me.

_____* <u>marital difficulties</u>.

_____* being too <u>nostalgic</u>, so I lose touch with the present.

_____* complications due to <u>overindulgence</u> in amusements.

_____* so much <u>sensual indulgence</u> that my health, happiness, or success is damaged.

_____* sexual activities that are disapproved of by my community.

_____* urinary tract disorders.

_____* venereal diseases (STDs).

_____* my lifestyle leading me toward wasting diseases.

_____SUBTOTAL 6-B

~~~

TOTAL: _____ (Sum of subtotals A plus B)

SCORING: Multiply total by 2 for Score 6.

TOTAL:_____

X ____2

SCORE = _____

ES6/Venus: **RECORD SCORE 6 HERE:**_____

Copy this score to page 99.

ASSESSMENT: ENERGY SYSTEM 7/SATURN

ES7/Saturn -- 7-A: **GOOD QUALITIES**.

Score on a scale of 0 to 5.

> Think about how these qualities affect your happiness. Then finish the sentences under the RATING GUIDE.
> - **Zero** means you <u>have enough</u> of this quality. You do NOT need more for your life to function well.
> - <u>Three</u> means you don't need much but you aren't suffering much from a lack.
> - <u>Five</u> means you <u>need more</u> of this quality for your life to function well.

RATING GUIDE					
0	1	2	3	4	5
|------------	---------------	---------------	--------------	---------------	
I have enough...		Maybe I need a little more...			I need more...

Rating | Quality

_____* ability to be <u>authoritative</u> with others.

_____* ability to <u>commit</u> myself to something I value.

_____* ability to <u>concentrate</u>.

_____* <u>care to conserve resources</u> for my life to succeed.

_____* <u>consistency</u> in order to succeed.

_____* <u>dignity</u> to be a success.

_____* <u>discretion</u> to make my life work well.

_____* attention to <u>duties</u> for my life to succeed.

_____* ability to <u>endure</u> to make my life a success.

_____* <u>frugality</u> for my life to succeed.

_____* <u>humility</u> to be really successful.

_____* <u>industrious habits</u> to make my life work well.

_____* ability to <u>keep secrets</u> to succeed.

_____* ability to match the <u>moral standards</u> of my community for my life to run smoothly.

_____* <u>perseverance</u> in order to succeed.

_____* <u>practicality</u> for my life to succeed.

_____* <u>prudent</u> decision-making in order to succeed.

_____* <u>realistic</u> expectations, thinking, and behavior to succeed and appreciate success.

_____* ability to take <u>responsibility</u> in order to succeed.

_____* <u>ruggedness</u> to succeed in life.

_____* <u>self-control</u> in order to succeed.

_____* <u>self-discipline</u> to reach success

_____* <u>stability</u> to make my life work well.

_____**SUBTOTAL 7-A**

~~~

ES7/Saturn -- 7-B: **PROBLEMS.**

Score on a scale of 0 to 5.

> Think about how these issues affect your happiness. Then finish the sentences under the RATING GUIDE.
> - <u>Zero</u> means you <u>have no problems with this issue</u>. You do NOT need help for your life to function well.
> - <u>Three</u> means you may have some difficulties but you aren't suffering greatly from them.
> - <u>Five</u> means you <u>need to resolve this issue</u> for your life to function well.
>
> RATING GUIDE
>
> ```
> 0          1          2          3          4          5
> |----------|----------|----------|----------|----------|
> ```
> I have no problems with...   I have some problems with...
>   I have big problems with...

<u>Rating</u> | <u>Problem</u>

_____* <u>anxiety</u>.

_____* <u>arthritis</u>.

_____* <u>bad dreams</u> or <u>nightmares</u> that damage my quality of life.

_____* <u>bone diseases</u>.

_____* <u>chronic illness</u>.

_____* too many exposures to <u>death</u> in my life.

_____* <u>delays</u> in my plans, projects, and expectations.

_____* <u>depression</u>.

_____* <u>difficulties</u> of many kinds, in general, that frequently disrupt my life.

_____* pervasive <u>disappointments</u> in life.

_____* <u>diseases</u> related to or affected by <u>coldness</u> (from arthritis to frostbite).

_____* <u>doubt</u> that cripples my decision-making, confidence, or happiness.

_____* being <u>easily discouraged</u>.

_____* <u>eczema</u>.

_____* <u>fearfulness</u>.

_____* people suggesting that I'm <u>not generous</u> enough.

_____* <u>humiliations</u> that damage my quality of life or my happiness.

_____* <u>idleness</u> or <u>inactivity</u> that hampers my ability to succeed.

_____* <u>inhibitions</u> that cripple my success and happiness.

_____* being <u>isolated</u> in ways that damage my happiness or productivity.

_____* <u>lack of confidence</u> in myself or my prospects.

_____* <u>laziness</u>.

_____* <u>lethargy</u> that damages my success.

_____* <u>loneliness</u>.

_____* <u>melancholy</u> that damages my life quality.

_____* general <u>misfortunes</u> in too many areas of life.

_____ * <u>paralysis</u>, mental, emotional or physical.

_____ * <u>physical pain</u>, especially bones, muscles, ligaments, joints.

_____ * <u>poverty</u>.

_____ * being too <u>resigned</u>, such that it damages my ability to succeed in what I might want.

_____ * being too <u>rigid</u> mentally or physically.

_____ * <u>shame</u> that interferes with my success or happiness.

_____ * <u>skin diseases</u>.

_____ * being too <u>suspicious</u> of other people or situations.

_____ * <u>timidity</u> that hampers my success or happiness.

_____ * being <u>unstable</u> mentally, or in the way I conduct my life.

_____ * <u>wasting diseases</u>.

_____ **SUBTOTAL 7-B**

~~~

TOTAL:_____ (Sum of subtotals A plus B)

SCORING: The total equals the score for ES7.
No calculation is necessary.

ES7/Saturn: **RECORD SCORE 7 HERE:**_____

Copy this score to page 99.

ASSESSMENT: ENERGY SYSTEM 8/RAHU
MOON'S NORTH NODE

ES8/Rahu -- 8-A: **GOOD QUALITIES**.
Score on a scale of 0 to 5.

Think about how these qualities affect your happiness. Then finish the sentences under the RATING GUIDE.

- **Zero** means you **have enough** of this quality. You do NOT need more for your life to function well.
- **Three** means you don't need much but you aren't suffering much from a lack.
- **Five** means you **need more** of this quality for your life to function well.

RATING GUIDE					
0	1	2	3	4	5
|------------|---------------|---------------|---------------|---------------|
I have enough...		Maybe I need a little more...		I need more...	

Rating | Quality

_____* courage to be happy and successful.

_____* detachment from personal or emotional situations for my life to work more smoothly.

_____* creativity to make my life a success.

_____* heightened awareness to make my life truly happy and successful.

_____* imagination to succeed.

_____* independence to be happy and fulfilled.

_____* individuality to be happy and successful.

_____* <u>insightfulness</u> to be happy and fulfilled.

_____* <u>originality</u> to feel fulfilled and successful.

_____* ability to <u>perceive the truth</u>.

_____* <u>popularity</u> to be happy.

_____* <u>self-fulfillment</u> to be happy in life.

_____* <u>surprises</u> for my life to be happy and fulfilling.

_____* <u>uniqueness</u> in the way I go about things in order to be fulfilled.

_____**SUBTOTAL 8-A**

~~~

ES8/Rahu -- 8-B: **PROBLEMS**. Score on a scale of 0 to 5.

Think about how these issues affect your happiness. Then finish the sentences under the RATING GUIDE.
- <u>Zero</u> means you <u>have no problems with this issue</u>. You do NOT need help for your life to function well.
- <u>Three</u> means you may have some difficulties but you aren't suffering greatly from them.
- <u>Five</u> means you <u>need to resolve this issue</u> for your life to function well.

RATING GUIDE

0	1	2	3	4	5

| -------------- | --------------- | --------------- | --------------- | -------------- |

I have no problems with...   I have some problems with...

I have big problems with...

<u>Rating</u> | <u>Problem</u>

_____* <u>addictions</u>.

_____* <u>anxiety</u> that cripples me.

_____* <u>confusion</u> that interferes with my success.

_____* being too close to <u>drownings</u> in my life.

_____* tendencies to <u>escapism</u> that interfere with my life.

_____* being too <u>gullible</u>.

_____* <u>hallucinations</u>.

_____* trusting <u>illusions</u> that end up disappointing me.

_____* being <u>imprisoned</u> in my life, literally or metaphorically.

_____* high <u>mental stress</u>.

_____* neuroses.

_____* psychoses.

_____* suffering as a result of <u>seeing only what I wanted to</u> <u>see</u>.

_____* being frequently <u>shocked</u> by others or circumstances.

_____* <u>timidity</u> that hinders my happiness or success.

_____* <u>vagueness</u>, either from myself or in others' expectations of me.

_____**SUBTOTAL 8-B**

~~~

TOTAL:_____ (Sum of subtotals A plus B)

SCORING: Multiply total by 2 for Score 8.

TOTAL:_____

X_____**2**

SCORE = _____

ES9/Rahu: **RECORD SCORE 8 HERE:**_____

Copy this score to page 99.

ASSESSMENT: ENERGY SYSTEM 9/KETU
MOON'S SOUTH NODE

ES9/Ketu -- 9-A: **GOOD QUALITIES**.
Score on a scale of 0 to 5.

> Think about how these qualities affect your happiness. Then finish the sentences under the RATING GUIDE.
> - <u>Zero</u> means you <u>have enough</u> of this quality. You do NOT need more for your life to function well.
> - <u>Three</u> means you don't need much but you aren't suffering much from a lack.
> - <u>Five</u> means you <u>need more</u> of this quality for your life to function well.

RATING GUIDE					
0	1	2	3	4	5
|------------	|--------------	|---------------	|-------------	|---------------	|
I have enough...		Maybe I need a little more...		I need more...	

Rating | Quality

_____* <u>compassion</u> for others to respect me.

_____* <u>idealism</u> to make my life happy and productive.

_____* ability to be <u>impressed</u> by people and circumstances around me.

_____* <u>intuition</u> to be happy and successful.

_____* ability to make <u>sacrifices</u> for others, in order to be happy and respected.

_____* <u>spiritual dedication</u> directed toward spiritual liberation (*moksha*).

_____* <u>spirituality</u> in my general outlook on life.

_____* <u>wisdom</u> as a result of experiencing challenges.

_____SUBTOTAL 9-A

~~~

ES9/Ketu -- 9-B: **PROBLEMS**. Score on a scale of 0 to 5.

Think about how these issues affect your happiness. Then finish the sentences under the RATING GUIDE.

- <u>Zero</u> means you <u>have no problems with this issue</u>. You do NOT need help for your life to function well.
- <u>Three</u> means you may have some difficulties but you aren't suffering greatly from them.
- <u>Five</u> means you <u>need to resolve this issue</u> for your life to function well.

RATING GUIDE

```
0           1           2           3           4           5
|-----------|-----------|-----------|-----------|-----------|
I have no problems with...        I have some problems with...
                                  I have big problems with...
```

<u>Rating | Problem</u>

_____* frequent <u>abscesses</u>.

_____* a tendency to be involved in too many <u>accidents</u>.

_____* <u>addictive behaviors.</u>

_____* criticism because I don't follow the <u>moral standards</u> of my community.

_____* <u>anger</u> — either losing my temper or being the target of others' anger.

_____* <u>colic</u> and similar stomach upsets.

_____* being too <u>eccentric</u> to succeed with my goals.

_____* carrying too much <u>emotional tension</u>.

_____ * <u>explosive</u> emotions, either my own or others', or actual <u>explosions</u> occurring too often in my life.

_____ * being so <u>fanatical</u> that it interferes with my happiness or success.

_____ * <u>fear complexes</u> that hinder my ability to move forward in life.

_____ * <u>hidden enemies</u> who undermine my success and happiness.

_____ * <u>hunger</u>, or not getting the proper nutrition.

_____ * being so <u>iconoclastic</u> (tendency to tear down others' revered beliefs) that it interferes with my success and happiness.

_____ * <u>impatience</u> that damages my success, happiness, or productivity.

_____ * being so <u>impulsive</u> that I often look back and wish I'd thought things out more carefully.

_____ * <u>inconsistency</u> that damages my success and happiness.

_____ * <u>insanity</u> — either my own or in those close to me.

_____ * <u>irritability</u> that reduces my quality of life.

_____ * too much <u>isolation</u>.

_____ * <u>mental disorders</u> that damage my quality of life.

_____ * <u>nightmares</u>.

_____ * <u>obsessive and compulsive behaviors</u>.

_____* skin diseases.

_____* being so <u>unconventional</u> that it interferes with my success and quality of life.

_____* too much <u>violence</u> in my life.

_____SUBTOTAL 9-B

~~~

TOTAL:_____ (Sum of subtotals A plus B)

SCORING: Multiply total by 2 for Score 9.

TOTAL:_____

X____2

SCORE =_____

ES9/Ketu: RECORD SCORE 9 HERE:_____

Copy this score to page 99.

ASSESSMENT: ENERGY SYSTEM 10/URANUS

ES10/Uranus -- 10-A: **GOOD QUALITIES**.

Score on a scale of 0 to 5.

> Think about how these qualities affect your happiness. Then finish the sentences under the RATING GUIDE.
> - <u>Zero</u> means you <u>have enough</u> of this quality. You do NOT need more for your life to function well.
> - <u>Three</u> means you don't need much but you aren't suffering much from a lack.
> - <u>Five</u> means you <u>need more</u> of this for my life to function well.

RATING GUIDE					
0	1	2	3	4	5
|------------	|---------------	|---------------	|---------------	|---------------	|
I am...		Maybe I should be a little more...		I should be more...	

<u>Rating</u> | <u>Quality</u>

_____ * <u>ahead of my time</u> to be really successful.

_____ * <u>creative</u> for my life to work out for the best.

_____ * <u>excited</u> for my life to be happier.

_____ * <u>flexible</u> for my life to work more smoothly.

_____ * aware of my own <u>freedom</u> to enhance my quality of life.

_____ * of a <u>genius</u> for my life to really work well.

_____ * <u>independent</u> in order to be happy and fulfilled.

_____ * <u>inspired</u> to make my life the best it can be.

_____ * <u>original</u> to have the life I want.

_____* <u>technologically adept</u> to get the most out of life.

_____* <u>thrilled with life</u> to be really happy.

_____**SUBTOTAL 10-A**

~ ~ ~

ES11/Uranus -- 10-B: **PROBLEMS.**

Score on a scale of 0 to 5.

Think about how these issues affect your happiness. Then finish the sentences under the RATING GUIDE.

- <u>Zero</u> means you <u>have no problems with this issue.</u> You do NOT need help for your life to function well.
- <u>Three</u> means you may have some difficulties but you aren't suffering greatly from them.
- <u>Five</u> means you <u>need to resolve this issue</u> for your life to function well.

RATING GUIDE

| 0 | 1 | 2 | 3 | 4 | 5 |

|--------------|--------------|--------------|--------------|--------------|

I have no problems with...   I have some problems with...

I have big problems with...

<u>Rating</u> | <u>Problem</u>

_____* too many <u>accidents</u> in my life.

_____* an inability to <u>commit</u> to people or projects, so that it damages my quality of life.

_____* getting involved in activities that are <u>disapproved</u> of by my community.

_____* <u>erratic behavior</u> (mine or others') that damages my quality of life.

_____* <u>insomnia</u>.

_____* <u>irritability</u> that compromises my happiness.

_____* <u>nervousness</u> that interferes with my sense of well-being.

_____* <u>restlessness</u> that interferes with my productivity and peace of mind.

_____* too many <u>upheavals</u> in my life.

_____SUBTOTAL 10-B

~~~

TOTAL:_____ (Sum of subtotals A plus B)

SCORING: Multiply total by 3 for Score 10.

TOTAL:_____

X_____**3**

SCORE =_____

ES10/Uranus: **RECORD SCORE 10 HERE:**_____

Copy this score to page 99.

ASSESSMENT: ENERGY SYSTEM 11/NEPTUNE

ES11/Neptune -- 11-A: <u>GOOD QUALITIES</u>.

Score on a scale of 0 to 5.

> Think about how these qualities affect your happiness. Then finish the sentences under the RATING GUIDE.
> - <u>Zero</u> means you <u>have enough</u> of this quality. You do NOT need more for your life to function well.
> - <u>Three</u> means you don't need much but you aren't suffering much from a lack.
> - <u>Five</u> means you <u>need more</u> of this quality for your life to function well.

RATING GUIDE					
0	1	2	3	4	5
|------------|---------------|---------------|---------------|---------------|
I have enough...		Maybe I need a little more...		I need more...	

<u>Rating</u> | <u>Quality</u>

_____* <u>compassion</u> so that my life is enhanced.

_____* personal <u>connection with spirit</u> to enrich my life experience.

_____* <u>imagination</u> to make my life fun.

_____* ability to be <u>"in tune with"</u> the present moment.

_____* <u>intuition</u> to make my life function effectively.

_____* <u>musical ability</u> to enhance the quality of my life.

_____* <u>psychic ability</u> to enhance my life.

_____* appreciation of <u>religion</u> to enhance the quality of my life.

_____* sense of the <u>romantic </u>to fully enjoy life.

_____* <u>sensitivity</u> to people and situations to help my life
move smoothly.

_____* <u>spiritual awareness</u> to feel fulfilled.

_____**SUBTOTAL 11-A**

~ ~ ~

ES11/Neptune -- 11-B: **PROBLEMS**.

Score on a scale of 0 to 5.

Think about how these issues affect your happiness. Then finish the sentences under the RATING GUIDE.

- <u>Zero</u> means you <u>have no problems with this issue</u>. You do NOT need help for your life to function well.
- <u>Three</u> means you don't have some difficulties but you aren't suffering greatly from them.
- <u>Five</u> means you <u>need to resolve this issue</u> for your life to function well.

RATING GUIDE

```
0          1          2          3          4          5
|--------------|--------------|--------------|--------------|--------------|
I have no problems with...        I have some problems with...
                                       I have big problems with...
```

<u>Rating</u> | <u>Problem</u>

_____* <u>addictions</u>.

_____* <u>alcoholism</u>.

_____* <u>co-dependency</u>.

_____* <u>drug dependencies</u>.

_____* negative <u>drug interactions</u>.

_____* <u>misdiagnoses of illnesses</u>.

_____* consequences of <u>misleading</u> other people, or being <u>misled</u>.

_____* being <u>out of touch with reality</u>.

_____* consequences of <u>seeing only what I want to see</u> and acting on it, to my later disappointment.

_____**SUBTOTAL 1-B**

~~~

TOTAL:_____ (Sum of subtotals A plus B)

SCORING: Multiply total by 3 for Score 11.

TOTAL:_____

X_____3

SCORE =_____

ES11/Neptune: **RECORD SCORE 11 HERE:**_____

Copy this score to page 99.

ASSESSMENT: ENERGY SYSTEM 12/PLUTO

ES12/Pluto -- 12-A: **GOOD QUALITIES**.

Score on a scale of 0 to 5.

> Think about how these qualities affect your happiness. Then finish the sentences under the RATING GUIDE.
> - <u>Zero</u> means you <u>have enough</u> of this quality. You do NOT need more for your life to function well.
> - <u>Three</u> means you don't need much but you aren't suffering much from a lack.
> - <u>Five</u> means you <u>need more</u> of this quality for your life to function well.

RATING GUIDE					
0	1	2	3	4	5
|------------|------------|------------|------------|------------|					
I have enough...		Maybe I need a little more...		I need more...	

<u>Rating</u> | <u>Quality</u>

_____ * <u>ability to heal</u> myself and others.

_____ * <u>charisma</u>.

_____ * ability to <u>concentrate</u>.

_____ * <u>deep wisdom</u> so my life is meaningful.

_____ * <u>extreme wealth</u> to accomplish my goals.

_____ * <u>growth orientation</u> to stay interested in life.

_____ * ability to <u>focus</u> in order to succeed.

_____ * <u>mastery of a specific subject</u> in order to succeed in a meaningful way.

_____ * power of <u>rejuvenation</u> to keep my life on track.

_____* predisposition to being <u>powerfully self-driven</u> to succeed in life.

_____* <u>transformation ability</u> for my life to be meaningful.

_____**SUBTOTAL 12-A**

~~~

ES12/Pluto -- 12-B: **PROBLEMS**.

Score on a scale of 0 to 5.

Think about how these issues affect your happiness. Then finish the sentences under the RATING GUIDE.

- <u>Zero</u> means you <u>have no problems with this issue</u>. You do NOT need help for your life to function well.
- <u>Three</u> means you don't have some difficulties but you aren't suffering greatly from them.
- <u>Five</u> means you <u>need to resolve this issue</u> for your life to function well.

RATING GUIDE

0	1	2	3	4	5

|-------------|---------------|--------------|--------------|--------------|

I have no problems with...   I have some problems with...

I have big problems with...

<u>Rating</u> | <u>Problem</u>

_____* being told I (or thinking I) <u>abuse positions of power</u>, or I am abused by those in a position of power.

_____* consequences of my belief that the <u>ends justify the means</u>.

_____* <u>interpersonal relationships</u> in which I am accused of being (or I am) abusive, or in which I'm abused by others.

_____* consequences of trying to <u>get even</u>, or with others seeking <u>revenge</u> against me.

_____* being accused of <u>manipulating</u> others, or I am <u>manipulated</u> by others.

_____* becoming <u>obsessed</u> with an issue, to the detriment of my success or quality of life.

_____* <u>total upheavals</u> in my life.

_____* frequently encountering <u>unfair conditions</u> or situations.

_____* being <u>victimized</u>.

_____**SUBTOTAL 12-B**

~~~

TOTAL:_____ (Sum of subtotals A plus B)

SCORING: Multiply total by 3 for Score 12.

TOTAL:_____

$$X \underline{\qquad 3}$$

SCORE =_____

ES12/Pluto: **RECORD SCORE 12 HERE:**_____

Copy this score to page 99.

---

7. EXAMINING YOUR SCORES

By listing your scores for each of the ESs, you can see which of your energies needs support. The highest scores need the most work, so select the only one or two highest scores to begin.

Score 1: _____

Score 7: _____

Score 2: _____

Score 8: _____

Score 3: _____

Score 9: _____

Score 4: _____

Score 10: _____

Score 5: _____

Score 11: _____

Score 6: _____

Score 12: _____

This information is a diagnosis of the energies that need balancing in your life. There may be several ESs with very high scores or only one or two that stand out. You may be highly motivated to change everything at once; tempted to tackle all the problems you see with all the tools at your disposal. That way lies burnout. It is best to choose one or two ESs and select one activity to start with. Once you get in the groove, you can add more.

Here is a place to list the ESs you will address first:

_____

_____.

NOTE TO JYOTISHIS

The next few paragraphs provide additional information to practitioners of Jyotish, or the Vedic "science of light." If you study or work with this system, the information below will provide more details in diagnosing a person's energy systems. If you are not a student of Jyotish, you can skip this section.

The scoring system in this book is based on the *karakas*, or associations, for each of the planetary Energy Systems. Supporting *karakas* is a basic tool for energy balancing. Additionally, when analyzing a Vedic birth chart, you may find other planets that need support. However, the first item of importance is to support the Ascendant and the Ascendant ruler (usually called the Ascendant <u>lord</u>). The Ascendant's strength is necessary for anything to get off the ground in life. It represents one's vitality, and if that is compromised, it doesn't matter how much talent or luck one has. The individual will simply not have the energy to accomplish anything. If the Ascendant ruler is weak, you will get only moderate results from other *upayas*. How do you know if the Ascendant is weak? It is weak...

> ➤ if the <u>*Ascendant*</u> contains or is aspected by malefic planets (Saturn, Mars, Rahu, Ketu), or the lords of the *sixth-*, *eighth-* and *twelfth-*houses). In these cases, the Ascendant lord and the difficult planet must both be balanced.

> ➤ if the Ascendant <u>*lord*</u> is conjunct or aspected by a difficult planet (Saturn, Mars, Rahu, Ketu, or the lords of the *sixth-*, *eighth-* and *twelfth-*houses). Here the Ascendant lord and the difficult planet must both be balanced.

> ➤ When looking at the *sixth-*, *eighth-*, and *twelfth-*houses, be sure to count house positions not only from the Ascen-

dant, but also from counting the Sun's position and the Moon's position as house ONE.

~~~

The next step is to listen for the "presenting issue:" What problem is this person attempting to resolve? Look for the house ruling this issue and the lord of this house. In a chart, planets that rule the *sixth-, eighth-, eleventh-* and *twelfth-*houses have the potential to cause harm.

➤ You don't want these rulers associated with the subject at hand. If the subject is "children", you don't want the rulers of *six, eight, eleven* or *twelve* conjunct the *fifth* lord (children), or in the *fifth-*house, or aspecting the *fifth-*house or the *fifth-*house lord.

➤ You don't want the ruler of the subject at hand to fall IN the *sixth-, eighth-,* or *twelfth-*houses, unless those houses ARE the subject at hand. (The ruler of the *sixth-*house IN the *sixth* protects the health.)

  ▪ *For example,* if the ruler of the *fifth-*house is in the *twelfth-*house, this could result in the loss of a child or the loss of an opportunity for a child (only if there are additional indicators that suggest those outcomes).

  ▪ *For example,* if the ruler of the *tenth-*house of career is in the *eighth-*house of bankruptcy and breaks in patterns, there may be recurring difficulties with the career. In this case, balancing the *tenth-*house ruling planet will enhance the strength of the career, and balancing the *eighth-*house ruling planet will help remove difficulties to the career.

> In addition, if the ruler of any house is debilitated, or conjunct or aspected by a malefic planet (Saturn, Mars, Rahu, Ketu), those conditions will cause difficulties to the subject of that house.

  - For example, if the ruler of the *tenth*-house is debilitated, the career will have difficulty getting off the ground. In such cases, balancing the ruling planet will enhance the life condition.

> Look also at the divisional chart (*varga*) ruling the issue (*e.g.,* for children that would be the *Saptamsa*).

> Be sure to examine the character and disposition of the *dasa* lord. It is generally useful to balance the energies of the *dasa* lord for best results during its period. This is even more important if that planet shows difficulties in the chart.

FOR WESTERN ASTROLOGERS

If you are a not a western astrologer you can skip this section. If you are, and don't want to learn a completely new system you can, with a few modifications, use the above rules to help you identify energy imbalances.

First, you will need to run a different chart so that the houses referenced above accurately reflect the energies of the individual. The Vedic system is based on the sidereal zodiac, which is about 23-24 degrees earlier than the tropical zodiac used by western astrologers. To apply this system you will need to set your astrology software to do the following:

> Use the SIDEREAL zodiac rather than the tropical zodiac. This drops the zodiac back 23-24 degrees.

> Use WHOLE SIGN HOUSES. It doesn't matter if the Ascendant degree is 6, or 26. WHOLE SIGN HOUSES

mean that each house completely contains one sign of the zodiac, from 0 degrees through 29 degrees.

➢ When examining aspects, first consider all conjunctions and oppositions. If you want additional detail, here are the rules:

- For Jupiter, also consider the planets and houses it trines.

- For Mars, also consider Mars' opening square and its eighth-house quincunx to other planets and houses.

- For Saturn, also consider its opening sextile and its closing square to other planets and houses

- For the nodes, also consider planets and houses they trine.

➢ If your program gives you the option, calculate the *dasas*. *Dasas* are the Vedic system of "Time Lords:" during each part of a person's life, one of the traditional planets will dominate his or her experience. These periods are of varying length and represent emotional or life-circumstance "climate changes" for the individual.

- Once you know the *dasa* lord (or "*dasa* ruler") for the current period, analyze the condition of that planet. Check to see if it's placed in "good" or "bad" houses and if it has aspects from benefic or from malefic planets.

- Use the *Vimshottari Dasa* system.

~~~

You may notice that some of the "correspondences" for the planetary energy systems are different than what is used in western tropical astrology. For example, in Vedic astrology Mars rules siblings and Jupiter rules your children. The energy balancing protocols used in this handbook are based on the Vedic system of energy correspondences.

For all the rest of your analysis, continue to use the systems you are accustomed to using. Use the sidereal chart to identify problem areas and recommended solutions.

PART III:

Balancing Energies

Illustration 4

Lucifer's Fall

SILK TAPESTRY BY ANNE BEVERSDORF
Based on a vision of HILDEGARD VON BINGEN.

In her vision, Hildegard saw Lucifer falling
almost as a leaf would fall from a plant.
This image is reminiscent of the *Mrityunjaya Mantra* which,
fitting the theme of Lucifer's Fall,
releases us from harm
"as a ripe fruit falls from the vine."

Color image viewable at:
http://www.sacred-threads.com/tapestries-2/hildegard-von-
bingen-inspired/lucifers-fall

"Lucifer's Fall"

"Lucifer's Fall"

8. PRINCIPLES FOR BALANCING ENERGIES

Three main categories of activity can balance energies. These are charity, prayer and ritual. Obviously, many people engage in charity, prayer and ritual in their daily lives without fixing their life's problems. If you need to balance ES7/Saturn, it will not help you to offer food to mothers of small children. If you want to balance ES1/Sun, it will not help to give to beggars. Each ES will respond to a different kind of charity.

The purpose of these activities is to make friends with the ES that is causing difficulties. Think of a real life situation concerning a person who is bossy and difficult to please. How would the situation change if that person thought of you as a friend? This attitude anthropomorphizes the ESs as a way to remind us that there can be good uses for difficult energies. You may not like angry people around you, yet in a milder form, anger is the same ES as the ability to move forward with purpose. So if you befriend the system that brings you anger (ES3/Mars) you also encourage the good use of assertiveness, a different form of that energy. As teacher and Jyotishi Hart de Fouw says, "Even Genghis Kahn was good to those who sucked up to him." You can befriend even the most difficult energies, making them "like you" and treat you well.

THE PATTERN

The key to designing a balancing exercise is to know three specific things and learn to mix and match these elements to create a pattern. The ultimate choices can be based entirely on your preferences.

You need to know:

1. The Energy System that needs balancing;

2. The day of the week strongest for that system; and

3. The colors, people, places, *mantras* and prayers associated with that ES.

In this section, you will find information about each ES in a table which lists the archetypal correspondences for that ES. These correspondences include categories of things related to the specific ES: the kinds of people (*e.g*, police, mothers, merchants, *etc*), the kinds of places (temples, sports arenas, playgrounds, *etc*), specific foods, plants, animals, specific grains, geometric shapes, and the names of gods, saints, and angels from a variety of religious traditions.

Your job will be to give SOMETHING from this list to SOME PLACE, SOME THING, or SOMEONE ELSE on this list. This needs to be done on the appropriate weekday for the ES. *Mantras* and prayers are given to God, so doing them counts both as prayer and as giving to God.

With this information, you can create activities that will balance your ESs and that will fit into your own lifestyle, schedule, and natural preferences. The same principles will guide you in performing rituals: you'll design rituals that mix the items associated with a specific ES. *Mantras* and prayers, likewise, must match the ES you're addressing.

For example, for ES1/Sun, your balancing activity could be:

> ➤ Day of the week: *Sunday*:

> ➤ Color and item associated with the Energy System: *red flowers*:

> ➤ Person associated with the Energy System: *father.*

Therefore, as an example, your balancing activity would be:

On Sundays, give red flowers to your father.

Alternately, on Sundays you could do a candle ritual by lighting a red candle and doing *mantras* or prayers for ES1/Sun, or you could do any number of other activities by mixing and matching items from the list for ES1/Sun.

As you study the balancing activities for each ES, you will discover there is a wide variety of activities available to you. You can do the same balancing activity every week, or you can swap activities each week, depending on your schedule and preferences.

> ➤ Start your activities on the appropriate weekday, unless an emergency requires you to start immediately.

> ➤ These activities must be repeated a minimum of nine weeks in a row for simple or passing issues.

> ➤ For large or long-term issues the activities must be repeated as many weeks as your age, plus one. Therefore, if you are 45 years old, you must perform the balancing activities for at least 46 weeks: *e.g.* your age, plus one week more.

➢ Remember, if you miss a week the count starts over from the beginning.

CHARITY AND SERVICE

The basic principle is to give to:

➢ one person, place, or symbol that is associated with the ES you are working with --

➢ an object that is also associated with the ES you're working with,

➢ on the day of the week associated with that ES,

➢ for the number of weeks required to balance the issue.

The Tables of Correspondences list many people, places, and things associated with each ES, which you can simply mix and match. (You will notice that some things will be listed under more than one Energy System.) Of course, the gift selected must be something valued by the receiver. For ES7/Saturn (Saturday), *trash* is one of the corresponding items and elderly people are corresponding persons. But an elderly person does not want trash on Saturday or any other day. This won't help. Instead, an excellent activity would be to take trash (or take an elderly person's trash) to a recycling center (that will appreciate receiving trash) on Saturday.

One simple charity is to give a flower of the appropriate color (be sure to remove any thorns first) to the "right" person represented by that ES on the "right" weekday. The "right" person and day are shown in the Table of Correspondences.

RITUALS

In a sense, any activity you do on a specific day over a period of time becomes a ritual. For our purposes, you will create very specific rituals designed to balance each ES. The most effective ones combine the ancient elements of Earth,

Fire, Air, Water and Ether. The key to designing your own is to include objects related to the ES on the correct day of the week, and then create a repeatable pattern.

As an example, look at the archetypal correlations to ES2/Moon. Objects would include rice, milk, and all forms of Mother (see the table for more). Colors are white and milky white. You could

> - create a space on the earth (EARTH ELEMENT) and

> - light a tiny fire (FIRE ELEMENT) of white paper (WHITE=ES2/MOON) in front of a

> - photo of your mother (ES2/MOON),

> - saying a prayer or *mantra* aloud (AIR ELEMENT),

> - or in your mind (ETHER ELEMENT);

> - then bury (EARTH)

> - a few grains of rice (RICE=ES2/MOON),

> - before quenching the fire with water (WATER.)

> - You could also include the shape that corresponds to the ES by drawing it with a stick in the dirt or sand,

> - or use grains to outline the shape on the ground (EARTH).

Candle Rituals

The easiest ritual is a candle ritual. This also includes the use of Earth/Air/Fire/Water/Ether. For about seven years of my life, I performed an easy daily candle ritual that seemed to smooth out rough edges for me. Here's exactly what I did, and you may want to try something similar:

> - I purchased seven long-burning devotional candles in glass jars. Most of the candles were unscented, but I

like to find a scented candle for ES6/Venus. These candles can be found in most supermarkets for about a dollar each.

➢ As time went on, I collected pictures representing important images associated with each ES and made myself a little card deck of these images.

➢ I also made a list of the seed *mantras* for each day, but soon didn't need that list anymore because most of them were short and easy to remember. [*Seed mantras* are syllables, not words, that create the vibratory essence of an Energy System.]

➢ I created an altar on top of a small chest of drawers, and kept the candles and other items for each ES in a series of dividers in the top drawer.

➢ Each day when I got up, I'd put the correct-colored candle on my altar and

- light it (FIRE),

- dunking the hot match in a tiny dish of EARTH for safety.

➢ Over time, I collected objects associated with each ES, and each morning would remove the previous day's candle and objects and move the picture associated with that day to the front of the deck. Then I'd take a few minutes to

- say the *mantra* (AIR). (For seed *mantras*, a full *mala* of 108 repetitions can be completed in less than two minutes.)

- I continued the *mantra* in my mind (ETHER) as I got dressed and ready for the day.

- Then, I would blow out the candle (AIR),

- pinch the wick with fingers dampened with WATER, and get on with the day.

For a while, I left the candle burning while I was at home (and since I work at home this was most of the time). However, this left a sooty spot on the ceiling, which turned out to be costly. When purchasing the candles for this ritual, remember that by lighting each candle for only a few minutes once a week, a single candle will last as long as a year.

I'm not sure this simple ritual made big changes in my physical life, as this was a difficult time for me. I am quite sure the equanimity I experienced then was uncharacteristic. It was also very much appreciated.

Fasting and Food Rituals

Each Table of Correspondences contains a list of foods associated with that Energy System. You can use this list in four ways:

➤ Go on a fast (with the permission of your medical advisor) on the weekday connected with the ES you are balancing.

➤ On the appropriate weekday, DO NOT eat any of the foods on the list FOR THAT ES. Instead, place samples on your altar or offer them (charity) to a person, place, or animal listed for that ES.

➤ Alternately, EAT several of the foods associated with that ES each week, particularly if these foods are not part of your regular diet. This is most effective when done with a prayer of appreciation for the ES (including people, places, *etc.*) you are balancing.

➤ Give quantities of food, or nice presentations of foods from the Table of Correspondences to a person (or place) from the Table on the appropriate weekday.

Other Rituals

Since each ES has a specific shape associated with it, the shape can be used to create another ritual.

➤ On the specific weekday,

➤ draw that shape on your altar, on your patio or front porch, or on your kitchen table or hearth ...

➤ using colored thread, or using the grain associated with that energy, or other items associated with that ES.

This is a form of honoring the energy you want to balance. You can also create a ritual by exposing drinking water to the Sun, using a transparent glass in a color that matches the ES you're working with. Then drink the water. This ritual is best for increasing good energies of a system— but REMEMBER, it can be DANGEROUS if you are already suffering from difficult manifestations of that Energy System. (If you have a trigger temper or frequently have accidents, you suffer from too much ES3/Mars. You don't want to drink in *more* of that energy!)

CREATIVE HOMAGE

This means honoring the ES with your own creativity.

➤ Draw, paint, dance, sing, write music, or do any other creative activity. Again, the key is to select the correct weekday and use elements from the Table of Correspondence as starting points for your creative work.

➤ Traditionally, people have painted complex pictures using, instead of sketched lines, the words of a prayer or *mantra*. These words are written in tiny script which substitutes for the lines a painter or illustrator would normally use. Imagine drawing the shape of Mickey Mouse's head with the iconic three circles, one for the head, two smaller ones for the ears. Now imagine drawing this in very pale pencil lines, and by using the words "MickeyMouseMickeyMouseMickey Mouse" in tiny letters, overwrite the pencil lines with words, so the Mickey Mouse head is created with the words of his name. Using full *mantras* to create the shapes (and even colored fillers) for your drawings is a potent form of creative homage. For the purposes of these exercises I'm calling this "*Mantra* Painting."

➤ Dress yourself or your environment in colors associated with the ES.

➤ Create dances.

➤ Write and perform puppet shows.

➤ Write mythologies based on traditional stories or

➤ Write new stories following the same basic themes as traditional mythologies.

➤ Sing and perform prayers and *mantras*.

There is literally no limit to the creative activity you can undertake to balance the ESs.

READ (OR WRITE) HEALING STORIES

Every spiritual tradition has stories that correspond to archetypal patterns. As Robert Svoboda, author of **The Greatness of Saturn,** points out, simply reading stories corresponding with the ES can help balance the system. Suggestions will be made under activities for the ESs, but there are many, many more stories than can be listed here.

MANTRAS AND PRAYERS

Mantras are usually in Sanskrit, although the meaning of "mantra" has expanded recently to include affirmations and prayers in any language. Sanskrit is considered one of the original languages, and sages believe that words spoken in Sanskrit express and manifest the physical reality of their meanings. This is the literal equivalent to the Biblical phrase, "In the beginning was the Word." When you repeat a mantra, you create a vibratory energy that becomes a part of you and enhances your own vibratory state, bringing qualities of that nature into your life.

Prayers are equally effective, especially prayers that have been repeated in the same way over many centuries. Any prayer, image of a saint or god, or affirmation that has been considered sacred and used by millions of people carries tremendous spiritual energy. So traditional forms of **The Lord's Prayer** or the **Doxology**, or **The 23rd Psalm**, or other material with a long tradition become especially potent for influencing ESs.

Specific customs relating to Sanskrit mantras can safely and easily be applied to prayers from other traditions.

➢ Each time you say a mantra or prayer, it should be repeated at least three times. This is the bare minimum.

➢ Repeating a mantra or prayer nine times in a single session is the effective minimum.

➢ It is best to do an entire mala (Indian prayer beads, similar to a rosary, but usually with 108 beads) of mantra repetition, which means 108 repetitions. With short mantras, this can easily be done within two or three minutes.

➢ With longer *mantras*, using prayer beads to count repetitions is helpful. *Rosaries* usually have 54 beads, and the Vedic prayer beads, or *malas* usually have 108.

➢ Singing a *mantra* aloud is a good way to learn it, yet the best way to use a *mantra* is to sing it in your mind. Sing it mentally so often that it gets "stuck" in your head like an advertising jingle or a popular song. This way it becomes a part of your own vibrational pattern. *Mantras* can be repeated "internally" instead of vocally.

The more often you repeat a *mantra* the more it becomes a part of you, so it gains effectiveness in enhancing your life.

I am not a Sanskrit scholar, and since Sanskrit does not use the English alphabet, there are many different English spellings of Sanskrit words. Scholars have special diacritical marks that indicate delicate and, to western ears, inaudible variations of pronunciations. I have spelled the *mantras* in ways that seem logical to me. When I write or say *mantras*, I always mentally apologize for my inadequate pronunciation and ask forgiveness, requesting that God make corrections for the errors I make. I offer the same apologies to you, and suggest you accompany your recitations with a request for spiritual "correction" and by acknowledging that these are your best, though imperfect, attempts.

When looking at the unfamiliar Sanskrit words, it is easy to become overwhelmed. The only way to pronounce them is

One - Syl - la - ble - At - A - Time.

For example, even the *name* of one of the most famous *mantras* is daunting: The MRITYUNJAYA *MANTRA*. Just take it one syllable at a time:

MRIT -- YUN -- JA -- YA.

121

You can download *FREE mp3 recordings* of many *mantras* in this book at www.stariel.com under the heading, Stariel Press. My pronunciation caveat applies to the recorded *mantras*. Nevertheless, it may be useful for you actually to hear the *mantras*.

PUJAS AND YAGYAS

The only activity here that costs more than pocket change is one that combines charity, prayer, and ritual. *Pujas* and *yagyas* are Hindu ceremonies specifically designed to address specific ESs. Performed by priests of the Vedic tradition, these ceremonies include both prayers and rituals, and requesting and paying for a *puja* or a *yagya* is also a charity that helps feed people who would otherwise go hungry.

While *pujas* include prayer and ritual, *yagyas* add the burning of a sacrificial fire to which objects associated with the ES are offered as gifts. For example, a *yagya* for ES6/ Venus, might include offering a beautiful sari to the fire, giving honor to representatives of the archetypal energies of this system.

Although these ceremonies are part of Hindu tradition, it is not necessary to be a Hindu to use them or to benefit from them. These traditions have been passed down for millennia. Historical researcher David Frawley makes a convincing case that they may be at least twelve thousand years old and may be source material for later religious ceremonies. It is possible to trace elements of other religions' rituals, including ancient Egyptian, Jewish, and even modern Christian rituals, to origins in the ancient Vedic system.

For those who are uncomfortable leaving their own religious tradition, it is possible to find correlations to the ES archetypes in most religions, and therefore to use your own religious ceremonies to honor the archetype through your own religion. In the Christian religion, honoring the Virgin

Mary would be a way of balancing ES2/Moon. You can find other correlations in the chapters on balancing each Energy System.

In my experience, there is a delicate balance between performing rituals from ancient patterns (*e.g., pujas, yagyas* and masses), and performing ad-hoc rituals to the same ES archetype with great sincerity and devotion. When a situation is critical, I will do both.

Sources for *Pujas* and *Yagyas*

There are two sources I recommend for *pujas* and *yagyas* done correctly and at reasonable prices. In both cases a single ceremony for a single ES will cost about $35.00.

1. www.puja.net is a cooperative started by my friend, Ben Collins. Ben, like me, saw the extraordinary prices charged by some providers of *pujas* and *yagyas*, and realized that they could be available to many more people if offered less expensively. Ben devised a cooperative for performing ceremonies which has been praised by the *Shankaracharyas* of India (a supreme religious leader, kind of like a pope). I scold Ben for not providing for his own financial needs as he arranges these services for others. He ignores my advice.

    One Puja.Net service offers multiple ceremonies each month for a single fee of $51/month. Since thousands of people participate, each person receives thousands of dollars of ceremonies during the month. When signing up, try to have your date, time, and place of birth available to customize the ceremony to your own energy. If your birth data is not available, the ceremonies are arranged to align with the energies at the time of your call, and are still useful.

2. www.amma.org is the contact point for Ammaji's pujas. You can learn more about the great Indian saint Amma at her website www.amma.org. Again, you will need your birth data, and the name of your "lunar nakshatra", which you can obtain from a jyotishi or from Vedic astrology software programs. Ammaji's pujas were my introduction to this system, and are conducted impeccably to great effect.

USING GEMSTONES

Many people are familiar with India's use of gemstones as remedies for difficult life situations. There are lists of gemstones included among the correlations to each ES. Generally, I don't recommend their use, because gemstones strengthen an ES <u>for good AND for ill</u>. For example, the same gemstone that increases your financial health could possibly damage the education of your children. An ES representing "growth" may sound like a good thing—unless you are battling the tumor growth of cancer. With gemstones, you'll get the bad with the good.

If you do venture into gemstone remedies, (and I confess my love for and experimentations with gemstones) be sure to use natural and preferably non-treated stones of as much clarity and size as you can obtain. It's more important to have clarity than a large size if you can't afford both. There is evidence that lab-created stones emphasize the worst aspects of the ES they represent. For example, a person using a gemstone remedy of emerald had a beautiful lab-created emerald set in a ring made according to strict Jyotish principles. He experienced nothing but nightmares the entire time he wore the ring. He took it off and the nightmares ceased. Another person using a lab-created blue sapphire ring reported <u>immediate</u> depression until the ring was removed. The only possible exception to this rule is pearls which, according to some, can be cultured or man-made without ill effect. The important point about pearls is that they be round and unblemished—not "baroque," or wrinkled, or oddly shaped.

If you really want to experiment with gemstones for balancing ESs be cautious, and then watch and observe your life carefully. Furthermore, if you are wearing a new gemstone and something starts going awry in your life, remove the jewelry and see if the situation improves.

There is another reason to avoid gemstone remedies. Those things that we do in life affect our karma for this life and for future lives. When we do activities and rituals to balance ESs, we take that balanced energy with us after death and actually increase the "good karma" in our multi-lifetime "karma pot."

A gemstone, on the other hand, is left behind with our physical body when we die. Its effect does not survive our death, and does not improve our karmic lot for the future. In Paramahamsa Yogananda's ***Autobiography of a Yogi***, Yogananda's teacher, Sri Yukteswar, prescribes for Yogananda the use of a gemstone for a brief period, for the sole purpose of saving his life. When that danger ended, he removed it.

REMINDERS:

To effectively balance Energy Systems in your life:

➢ You must do balancing activities every week, without a break, either for nine consecutive weeks or for the number of weeks equal to your age plus one more.

➢ The basic principle means doing ceremonies and/or prayers and *mantras*, and/or other activities that match the ES you are trying to balance.

➢ When doing balancing activities, include objects, people and places from that ES's archetypal correspondences.

125

➤ You don't have to do ALL the activities. Doing ONE activity is the best way to start. You can add more later if you want to. If you suspect your karma is very stuck, it would be good to add many activities, but always START WITH ONE.

➤ You don't have to do the same activity every week.

➤ You can vary the activity you choose in any way you wish that still relates to the Correspondences for that Energy System.

9. ACTIVITIES FOR BALANCING MATERIAL ENERGY SYSTEMS

Obviously, the Energy Systems used in this book are related to the names of the planets in our solar system. This is convenient, because planetary energies correspond to the great archetypes of mythologies around the world. Planetary archetypes function, linguistically, as cachepots for series' of archetypally related mythologies. For instance, where else can you quickly link the mythologies of Mercury, Hermes, Thoth, and Coyote with the complicated Vedic story of Mercury being the illegitimate son of Jupiter and the Moon? These myths are all archetypally related, and by using the planetary name, we can unite all these cultural histories in a single location.

Another reason to use planetary names is because astrologers understand the symbols of geometric relationships between these systems at a person's birth. Geometric relationships between Energy Systems provide even more information about balancing energies.

Few people realize that astrologers are just as baffled by how these systems work as the most ardent skeptic. Astrologers just know that day after day, year after year, when they apply the rigid principles and insights offered by archetypal understandings, they are able to gain profound insights and even predictive information about the lives of people they work with. Because we don't know how it works, the consistent results can be as amazing to the astrologer as to the client.

Until the 18th century, human understanding of the solar system was limited to the planets visible to the naked eye. In addition to the Sun and Moon, used by astrologers but technically termed "lights," instead of "planets," the visible planets include Mercury through Saturn. These are the only planets we can see using only our eyes. The discovery of more planets (and dwarf planets and trapped comets) thanks to telescopes, has expanded the catalog of our solar system. Since this expansion, astrological thinking now recognizes that "traditional planets," *e.g.* those visible to the naked eye, have the most to do with the physical world around us. This conclusion results from a kind of emotional and intuitive logic rather than scientifically measurable logic; the kind of logic that addresses issues of *meaning* in our lives, which is left unaddressed by scientific fact.

Themes addressed by these traditional Energy Systems tend to be the "nuts and bolts" issues of our lives. More often than not, such issues include physical health and well-being; our jobs; marriages; children; homes; parents; siblings; automobiles; and other external and physical manifestations of life. So, Energy Systems classified here as "Material Energy Systems" express themselves in very material ways.

By balancing the energies of these systems, you will find outer conditions of your life will evolve and change, but your feelings about them may not. For example, you may have a greater income, but still spend too much on gambling, or on new shoes, or you may still worry about not having "enough." You may also need to balance the Subtle and Transcendent Energy Systems (Chapters 10 and 11) to regain balance in all areas.

BALANCING ENERGY SYSTEM 1/SUN

ES1/SUN Table of Correspondences

SHAPE: Rectangle.

WEEKDAY: Sunday.

DIVINITIES: Agni, Divine Father, Higher Self, Christ, Rama,
             Krishna, Buddha, Vishnu, Mohammed, Shiva,
             Apollo, Archangel Michael.

PEOPLE: Kings, fathers, government officials, males,
            presidents, physicians, powerful people, high-
            class people.

PARTS OF BODY: Heart, spine, right eye, ring finger.

ANIMALS: Lions, tigers, deer, geese, glow-worms, fireflies,
          eagles, roosters.

PLANTS: Very large and strong trees, red flowers, large
            showy yellow flowers, marigolds, celandines,
            peonies, sunflowers, rare or expensive woods,
            (including orange trees, cedar, almond),
            lavender, medicinal herbs, aromatic herbs, pine
            trees, frankincense trees, cedar trees, laurel trees,
            citrus trees.

FOODS: Hot and spicy foods, cayenne, black pepper,
            ginger, cardamom, saffron, bayberry, cinnamon,
            calamus, camphor, eucalyptus, bitter foods,
            chamomile, almond, rosemary, nutmeg, fine
            wines, liquors, St. John's wort, oranges, citrus
            fruits.

PLACES: Temples, churches, open areas, deserts, palaces,
            fabulous buildings, government buildings (*e.g.*
            "The White House), home of the ruler, theaters.

GEMS AND MINERALS: Ruby, red spinel, red garnet, gold, copper.

GRAINS: Wheat.

COLORS: Deep red (preferred), yellow, gold, orange.

BALANCING ACTIVITIES

<u>Charity and Service</u> – Examples:

On Sundays, do one or more of the following activities:

➤ Give red flowers to government leaders.

➤ Give red flowers to your father

➤ Give red flowers to your doctor.

➤ Give fragrant herbs to a temple (or to government leaders, your father or to a doctor).

➤ Offer hot and spicy foods to an ES1/Sun person.

➤ Give wheat or copper in charity.

➤ Plant long-lived trees, or marigolds, peonies, sunflowers, or aromatic herbs in the yard of a temple or church. (Get permission).

➤ Join a project to plant trees in open areas.

➤ Give fireflies (or your painting of fireflies) to your father.

➤ Use the ES1/Sun Table of Correspondences to mix and match your own charity or service.

Candle Ritual — Example:

The following steps comprise an example of a candle ritual. As you become more familiar with the correspondences for ES1/Sun you may vary this process to better match your inclinations.

1. Light a red candle (FIRE) at dawn (or whenever you get up) on Sunday.

2. Tamp out the match in a dish of earth (EARTH).

3. Surround the candle with red flowers, red stones (EARTH), and images (statues or photographs) of Agni, Christ, Rama, Krishna, Buddha, Vishnu, Mohammed, Shiva, Apollo, Archangel Michael or any ES1/Sun archetype, which can include pictures of your own father or grandfather.

4. Use your breath (AIR) to express appreciation for ES1/Sun, requesting that only the most auspicious of its potentials affect your life (ETHER).

5. Repeat a simple ES1/Sun *mantra* or prayer (ETHER).

6. Dampen your fingers with water (WATER) (or use a stick) to pinch out the flame.

7. Release your breath and intention to the universe (ETHER).

Fasting and Food Rituals — Examples:

➢ Fast on nine consecutive Sundays (with the permission of your medical professional).

➢ On nine consecutive Sundays, or for nine consecutive days starting on Sunday, refrain from eating hot and spicy foods, ginger, cardamom, cinnamon, almonds, rosemary, nutmeg, fine wines, liquors, oranges, or any of the other foods related to ES1/ Sun.

➢ Give the above foods to ES1/Sun people in charity.

➢ Alternately, go out of your way to consume several of these foods on Sundays, particularly those foods that are not a normal part of your diet.

Other Rituals — Examples:

On Sundays, do one or more of the following activities:

➢ Use wheat grains (or wheat flour, or red string or yarn) to create the shape of a rectangle outside your front door, or on your candle altar. You can repeat *mantras* or add other ES1/Sun objects to this image.

➢ At dawn (or whenever you get up), fill a ruby-red, translucent glass with water and place it in the sunlight. On Sunday evening, drink the water to ingest ES1/Sun energies. (CAUTION: Do not do this if you suffer any of the problems of ES1/Sun.)

Creative Homage — Examples:

➢ On Sunday, draw, paint, sculpt, or do needlework to create an image of Agni, Christ, Rama, Krishna, Buddha, Vishnu, Mohammed, Shiva, Apollo, Archangel Michael or any of the ES1/Sun correspondences, also including government officials, presidents, a respected king, a physician, or your father.

➢ Create the above picture using *"Mantra* Painting" – writing tiny, curving ES1/Sun *mantras* in place of penciled lines and solid blocks of color.

➢ Use reds, oranges, golds and vivid yellow colors in your painting.

➢ Sing or silently say ES1/Sun prayers or *mantras* while you create.

➢ Compose and sing a song honoring the Sun or to something associated with ES1/Sun.

Healing Stories — Examples:

On Sundays, do one or more of the following activities:

➢ Read stories about God, Christ, Rama, Krishna, Buddha, Vishnu, Mohammed, Shiva, Apollo, Archangel Michael, great kings, presidents (biographies of Lincoln or FDR), or great doctors (like Albert Schweitzer or Alexander Fleming).

➢ Or write your own stories about these figures.

➢ Write stories about courageous lions, great Grandfather Trees, eagles, or about the wonderful and enduring history of a temple or religious site.

Mantras and Prayers:

From the different varieties of *mantra* and prayer below, select the version that addresses the conditions you are concerned with. While you may repeat these on any day of the week, be <u>sure</u> to do it on Sundays. When Sanskrit is available, use Sanskrit. Translations do not carry the same vibrational power.

Seed *Mantra*

OM Sum

Simple *Mantras*

- OM Suryaya Namaha   Dispeller of ignorance

- OM Savitra Namaha   Light of enlightenment

- OM Adityaya Namaha   Light of the Sage

- OM Ravaye Namaha   Light of compelling radiance

- OM Bhanave Namaha   Shining principle

- OM Pushne Namaha   Light of mystic fire

- OM Arkaya Namaha   Light that removes afflictions

  OM Mitraya Namaha   Light of universal friendship

Gayatri *Mantra*

OM bur buvah swaha
Tat Savitur varehnyam
Vargo devasya Dheemahi
Diyo yo na Prachodayat.

(translation)

Oh God! Giver of Life, Remover of pain and sorrow,
Bestower of happiness, Creator of the Universe,
May we receive thy supreme sin-destroying light,
May Thou guide our intellect in the right direction.

<u>Surya (Sun) Gayatri *Mantra*</u>

OM Bhaskaraye vidmahe
Divakraraye Dheemahi
Dhano Suryah Prachodayat.

(translation)

Let us meditate on the shining Sun god
Who gives light to the whole world.
May the Sun, who is the cause of day,
Inspire and illumine our mind and understanding.

Other *Mantra*

Japa kusuma Sankarsham
Kashyapeyam Mahadyutim
Tamorim Sarva Papaghnam
Pranato shmi Divakaram.

(translation)

Let us chant the glories of the Sun,
Whose beauty rivals that of a flower.
I bow down to him,
The greatly effulgent son of Kashyapa,
Who is the enemy of darkness
And destroyer of all sins.

The Lord's Prayer

Our Father, which art in heaven,
Hallowed be thy name.
Thy kingdom come, thy will be done,
On earth as it is in heaven.
Give us this day our daily bread,
And forgive us our trespasses,
As we forgive those who trespass against us.

Lead us not into temptation,
But deliver us from evil.
For Thine is the kingdom, the power
And the glory, forever.

Amen.

Doxology

Praise God from whom all blessings flow.
Praise Him all creatures here below.
Praise Him above, ye heavenly host.
Praise Father, Son, and Holy Ghost.

Amen.

Pujas and *Yagyas*

Contact www.puja.net or www.amma.org to arrange *pujas* or *yagyas.*

BALANCING ENERGY SYSTEM 2/MOON

ES2/MOON Table of Correspondences

SHAPE: Circle.

WEEKDAY: Monday.

DIVINITIES: Divine Mother, Parvati, Tara, Kwan Yin, Virgin
           Mary, Mary Magdalene, Archangel Gabriel,
           Demeter, Moon goddesses, Hecate, Selene,
           Artemis, Athena, Diana, Cerridwen.

PEOPLE: Mothers, the Queen, females, caregivers, nurses,
           nursery-workers (for plants, animals and
           children), food providers, hotel service persons,
           infants, the public at large, sailors, drunkards,
           midwives.

PARTS OF BODY: Stomach, breasts, digestive system, female
           organs, lymphatic system, left eye. On the hand,
           the Mount of Luna is on the lower part of the
           palm opposite the thumb.

ANIMALS: Antelope, rabbit, water-animals, partridge, crane,
           ducks, water birds, frogs, shellfish, fish.

PLANTS: White flowers, jasmine, gardenias, lotus, lilies,
           plants or trees that are oily or sappy, plants with
           milky sap, night-blooming plants, water-
           blooming plants, poppies, palm trees,
           sandalwood trees.

FOODS: Milk and milk products, melons, everyday fruits
           and vegetables, cucumbers, marshmallows,
           coconuts, slippery elms, comfrey roots, corn,
           Solomon's seal, mild herbs, water, beer, stewed
           or brewed foods, cold foods, tender or juicy

> fruits, salty flavors, fish, cabbages, onions, lettuce, mushrooms, tapioca pudding.
>
> PLACES: Watery places, aquariums, beaches, docks, rivers, oceans, wells, swamps, boats, ships, public places, hotels and motels, nests, waterside homes, breweries, dairies, hospitals, women's residences or dormitories, fountains.
>
> GEMS AND MINERALS: Pearls (round, not "nubby" or "baroque"), moonstones, silver, bronze, clear crystals, opals.
>
> GRAINS: White rice.
>
> COLORS: Milky-white (preferred), silver, pale and pastel colors.

BALANCING ACTIVITIES

Charity and Service -- Examples

On Mondays, do one or more of the following activities:

➢ Give white flowers (without thorns) to mothers of young children, to women's shelters, nurseries or child-care centers, or to your own mother.

➢ Give milk, powdered milk, or rice to mothers of young children, women's shelters, nurseries or child-care centers, or to your mother (if it would be appreciated).

➢ Throw pieces of silver in a river (fresh running water and silver belong to ES2/Moon).

➢ Place a clear glass of water under the moonbeams on a Monday night, and drink it Tuesday morning to ingest more of ES2/Moon.

➢ Give milk or milk products, melons, tapioca pudding, marshmallows, coconuts, beer, stewed or

brewed foods, fish, mushrooms, or other ES2/
Moon foods (only if they would be appreciated) to
women, caregivers, mothers of small children,
nurses, hotel service persons or other ES2/Moon
persons.

➢ Give water-blooming plants (with permission) to
aquariums, public ponds, waterside homes, hospi-
tals, hotels, or other ES2/Moon places.

➢ Plant white-blooming flowers in your kitchen garden, or in an ES2/Moon place (with permission).

➢ Donate milk, rice, or milk-cows or goats (or money
to buy them) to projects that feed mothers and
young children.

➢ Use the ES2/Moon Table of Correspondences to mix
and match your own charity or service.

Candle Ritual — Example:

The following steps comprise an example of a candle
ritual. As you become more familiar with the correspondences for ES2/Moon, you may vary this process to better
match your inclinations.

1. Light a white candle (FIRE) at dawn (or whenever
   you get up) on Mondays.

2. Tamp out the match in a dish of earth (EARTH).

3. Surround the candle with white flowers, pearls,
   milky quartz (EARTH), and images of the Virgin
   Mary, Artemis, Hecate, Cerridwen, Tara, Kwan Yin,
   Mary Magdalene, Archangel Gabriel, Demeter, Isis,
   Moon goddesses, or Divine Mother in any form, or
   your own mother or grandmother.

4. Use your voice (AIR) to express appreciation for
   nurturers. Express appreciation of the ES2/Moon

principles, requesting that only the most auspicious of its potentials affect your life (ETHER).

5. Repeat a simple ES2/Moon *mantra* or prayer (ETHER).

6. Dampen your fingers (or a stick) with water (WATER) to pinch out the flame.

7. Release your breath and intention to the universe (ETHER).

Fasting and Food Rituals — Examples:

➤ Fast on nine consecutive Mondays (with the permission of your medical professional).

➤ On nine consecutive Mondays, or on nine consecutive days starting on Monday, refrain from eating milk or milk products, melons, everyday fruits and vegetables, cucumbers, marshmallows, coconuts, slippery elm, comfrey root, corn, mild herbs, beer, stewed or brewed foods, cold foods, fish, cabbages, onions, lettuce, mushrooms or any of the foods related to ES2/Moon.

➤ Give the above foods to ES2/Moon people as charity.

➤ Alternately, go out of your way to consume several of these foods on Mondays, particularly those foods that are not a normal part of your diet.

Other Rituals — Examples:

➤ On <u>Sunday</u> nights, keep a clear glass of milk by your bed, and on Monday morning pour the milk on the ground below a palm tree, a night-blooming plant, melon plants, lotus, lily, jasmine, gardenia, or a plant or tree that is oily or sappy.

➤ On Mondays, use grains of white rice or use white string or yarn to create a circular shape on your altar, front porch, kitchen table, or kitchen counter. Use items from the ES2/Moon Table of Correspondences to complete your image. Say ES2 *mantras* and prayers over the image, or as you create it.

➤ Create a space on the earth (EARTH) and

- light a tiny fire (FIRE) of white paper (white= Moon) in front of a

- photo of your mother (ES2/Moon),

- saying a prayer or *mantra* aloud (AIR) or in your mind (ETHER);

- then bury (EARTH)

- a few grains of rice (rice=Moon),

- before quenching the fire with water (WATER).

- Include the shape that corresponds to the ES by drawing it with a stick in the dirt or sand.

- or use grains to outline the shape.

Creative Homage — Examples:

➤ On Mondays, draw, paint, sculpt, or create needle-work to make an image of the Virgin Mary, Mary Magdalene, Kwan Yin, Isis, Athena, Artemis, Hecate, Cerridwen, Tara, Demeter, the Archangel Gabriel, Moon goddesses, any image of Divine Mother, of your own mother or grandmother, Mother Theresa, or others who represent the concept of nurturing love to you.

➤ Create the above picture using *"Mantra* Painting," – writing tiny, curving ES2/Moon *mantras* in place of penciled lines and solid blocks of color.

➤ Use whites, milky whites, and pale, chalky pastel colors to create your image.

➤ Sing or silently say ES2/Moon prayers or *mantras* while you work.

➤ Compose and sing a song honoring the Moon or any of the persons or divine beings associated with ES2/Moon.

Healing Stories — Examples:

On Mondays, do one or more of the following activities:

> Read stories or biographies about the Virgin Mary, Mary Magdalene, Kwan Yin, Isis, Artemis, Diana, Hecate, Cerridwen, Athena, Demeter, Tara, the Archangel Gabriel, Moon goddesses, any image of Divine Mother, or of archetypal female nurturers like Mother Theresa, Florence Nightingale, *etc.*

> Or write your own stories about these figures, or about your mother or grandmothers.

> Create and produce puppet plays about small animals such as rabbits, partridges, cranes, ducks and other water birds, frogs, shellfish or fish.

> Write inspiring stories about a great aquarium, beautiful beach, sacred or magical wells, famous hotels, or historical fountains.

> Read *__Goodnight Moon__* by Margaret Wise Brown or other (age-appropriate) stories on the topics mentioned above to young children.

Mantras and Prayers:

From the variety below, select the version of the *mantra* or prayer that addresses the conditions you are concerned with. While you may repeat these any day of the week, be sure to do it Mondays. When Sanskrit is available, use Sanskrit. Translations do not carry the same vibrational power.

Seed *Mantras*

- Cham   (pronounced "chum")

- Shreem

- Som

Simple *Mantras*

- OM Sum Somaya Namaha.   Bliss and joy

- OM Chum Chandraya Namaha.   Stability

Mrityunjaya *Mantra*

Since a disturbed Moon causes emotional afflictions, the Mrityunjaya *Mantra* is especially good for restoring peace of mind.

OM, Tryumbakam yayamahe
Shugandhim pushti Vardhanam.
Urdvaru Kamiva Bandhanan
Mrityor, Mukshiya mam ritad.

(translation)

We meditate on Shiva
The three-eyed one of sweet fragrance,
Who expands spiritual growth.
Like the fully-ripened fruit
Drops from its stem,
May I be free from the bondage of death
And attachment in life,
But not from immortality.

Chandra/Soma (Moon) Gayatri

OM Padmadwajaya Vidmahe
Hema Roopaya Dheemahi,
Dhano soma Prachodayat.

(translation)

Let me meditate on the son of milk
Essence of nectar,
Let the Moon enlighten me.

Other *Mantras*

Dadhi shankha tusharabham
Kshirodarnava sambhavam
Namami shashinam somam
Sambhor mukuta bhushanam.

(translation)

I offer honor and respect to the Moon
Whose complexion resembles curds,
The whiteness of conch shells, and snow.
He is the ruling deity of the soma-rasa
Born from the Ocean of Milk,
And he serves as the ornament
On top of the head of Lord Shambhu.

147

<u>Prayer</u>

Hail Mary, full of grace,
The Lord is with thee.
Blessed art thou amongst women,
and blessed is the fruit of thy womb, Jesus.
Holy Mary, Mother of God,
Pray for us sinners,
Now and at the hour of our death.

Amen.

<u>*Pujas* and *Yagyas:*</u>

Contact www.puja.net or www.amma.org to arrange *pujas* or *yagyas.*

BALANCING ENERGY SYSTEM 3/MARS

ES3/MARS Table of Correspondences

SHAPE:	Hourglass.
WEEKDAY:	Tuesday.
DIVINITIES:	Mars/Aries, Bhumi, Mangala, Skanda (war god), Kartikeya, Archangel Samael, Saint George, Hercules.
PEOPLE:	Siblings, police, armed people, people who cut (surgeons, butchers, acupuncturists, tattoo artists, *etc.*), robbers, people who work with heat and metals, blacksmiths, farriers, military generals, barbers, soldiers, carpenters, athletic competitors. Also our physical senses and animal instincts.
PARTS OF BODY:	The head, muscles, blood, the triangle at the center of the palm.
ANIMALS:	Monkeys, jackals, rams, roosters, vultures, raptors, warlike and ravenous animals, mastiffs, wolves, leopards, bears, sharks.
PLANTS:	Red and orange flowers, nettles, thistles, brambles, mustard-seed, horehound, thorn trees, chestnut trees, hemlock, poison ivy and poison oak, hemp.
FOODS:	Radishes, tamarinds, leeks, onions, pungent flavors, mustard, peppers, coriander, garlic, coffee, tea, strong-smelling foods, heavy-protein foods, red meats, cinnamon, saffron, cayenne, black pepper, ginseng, astragalus, myrrh, turmeric, aloe, gentian, goldenseal, echinacea.
PLACES:	Landed property, home that one owns, places of fire, places of slaughter, combat zones, smiths

(e.g. blacksmiths, , silversmiths, *etc.*), furnaces, forges, battlegrounds, factories where fire and machinery are used, kitchens (hot ovens), boxing and wrestling rings, football stadiums, places popular with blue-collar workers, armories, military bases.

GEMS AND MINERALS: Red coral, carnelian, bloodstone, copper, gold, iron.

GRAINS: Red lentils.

COLORS: Reds, oranges, and fiery colors.

BALANCING ACTIVITIES

<u>Charity and Service</u> — Examples:

On Tuesdays, do one or more of the following activities:

- Give orange or red flowers to an ES3/Mars person, or to a battleground, communal kitchen, military base, athletic stadium or other ES3/Mars place.

- Throw sweet candies, or cinnamon "red-hots" in running water.

- Give copper (for example, old-fashioned pennies) to your sibling, a tattoo artist, acupuncturist, surgeon, someone who works with heat or metal, a barber, a butcher, a soldier, carpenter, athlete, or other person representing ES3/Mars.

- Clear poison ivy, oak, or poison sumac from a memorial battleground park.

- Give strong-smelling foods to a monkey, ram, vulture, mastiff, or other ES3/Mars animal.

- Use the ES3/Mars Table of Correspondences to mix and match your own charity or service.

Candle Ritual — Example:

The following steps comprise an example of a candle ritual. As you become more familiar with the correspondences for ES3/Mars, you may vary this process to better match your inclinations.

1. Light an orange or red candle (FIRE) at dawn (or whenever you get up) on Tuesday.

2. Tamp out the match in a dish of earth (EARTH).

3. Surround the candle with orange flowers, red and orange stones, (EARTH), and images (statues or photographs) of Mars/Aries, Archangel Samael, Bhumi, St. George, Hercules, Mangala, Skanda, Kartikeya, famous generals (Alexander the Great, General Patton, Hannibal, General Dwight Eisenhower), great athletes, and/or pictures of your own siblings or other ES3/Mars representatives.

4. Use your breath (AIR) to express appreciation for ES3/Mars requesting that only the most auspicious of its energies affect your life (ETHER).

5. Repeat a simple ES3/Mars *mantra* or prayer (ETHER).

6. Dampen your fingers (or a stick) with water (WATER) to pinch out the flame.

7. Release your breath and intention to the universe (ETHER).

Fasting and Food Rituals — Examples:

➤ Fast on nine consecutive Tuesdays (with the permission of your medical professional).

➤ On nine consecutive Tuesdays, or for nine consecutive days starting on Tuesday, refrain from eating radishes, leeks, onions, pungent foods, mustard, peppers, garlic, coffee, tea, strong-smelling foods, heavy-protein foods, red meats, cinnamon, and other foods related to ES3/Mars.

➤ Give the above foods to your siblings, to police or other people who carry weapons, people who cut skin -- like surgeons, butchers, acupuncturists, tattoo artists, and some nurses; barbers, competitive athletes, or other ES3/Mars people.

➤ Alternately, go out of your way to consume several of the above foods on Tuesdays, particularly those that are not a normal part of your diet.

Other Rituals — Examples:

On Tuesdays, do one or more of the following activities:

➤ Use red lentils or orange yarn to create the shape of an hourglass outside your front door, on your personal altar, your kitchen counter, your fireplace hearth, or patio. In addition, you can repeat an ES3/Mars *mantra* while you do this, and place ES3 items in and around the hourglass shape.

➤ In the morning, place an orange, translucent glass filled with water in the sunlight. Drink the water in the evening to ingest ES3/Mars. CAUTION: Do not do this if ES3/Mars is already overly strong in your life.

Creative Homage--Examples:

On Tuesdays, do one or more of the following activities:

➤ Draw, paint, sculpt, or do needlework to create an image of Mars, Aries, Hercules, Bhumi, Mangala, Skanda (or other war gods), Kartikeya, Archangel Samael, a portrait of your own sibling, of famous and respected military leaders or other ES3/ Mars people, or of a favorite piece of land that you own (including national parks).

➤ Create the above picture using "*Mantra* Painting," -- writing tiny, curving ES3/Mars prayers or *mantras* in place of penciled lines and solid blocks of color.

➤ Use oranges, reds, and other fiery colors in your work.

➤ Sing or silently say ES3/Mars prayers or *mantras* while you create.

➤ Using caution (this could strengthen both good and bad qualities of Mars) listen to marches or military bands, preferably marching or singing along with the music.

➤ Compose and sing a song honoring Mars, or honoring one of the persons or divine beings associated with ES3/Mars.

➤ Create songs, write plays, or create puppets representing people or animals of ES3/Mars.

Healing Stories — Examples:

On Tuesdays, do one or more of the following activities:

➤ Read stories or biographies about Mars, Skanda or other war gods, St. George, Hercules, Alexander the Great, General Patton, Hannibal, General Eisenhower, great athletes, or other representatives of ES3/Mars.

➤ Or write your own stories about the above figures.

➤ Write stories about blacksmiths, famous battles, famous athletic competitions, (or re-watch your favorite ballgame) or make up and write your own hero story.

Mantras and Prayers:

Select the version of the *mantra* that addresses the conditions you are concerned with. While you may repeat these on any day of the week, be sure to do it on Tuesdays. When Sanskrit is available, use Sanskrit. Translations do not carry the same vibrational power.

Seed *Mantras*

- OM Kum
- OM Am
- OM Mam
- OM Ram

Simple *Mantras*

- OM Kujaya Namaha.
  > Dispels disagreements

- OM Angarakaya Namaha.
  > Dispels aggressiveness

- OM Mangalaya Namaha.
  > Dispels destructiveness

Angaaraka (Mars) Gayatri

OM Veeradwajaya Vidmahe
Vighna Hasthaya Dheemahi
Dhano Bhauma Prachodayat.

(translation)

> Let me meditate on him who has heroes in his flag,
> He who has power to solve problems,
> Let the son-of-earth God enlighten me.

Other *Mantra*

Dharani Garbha Sambhutam
Vidyut Kanti samaprabha
Kumaram Shakti hastam cha
Mangalam Pranamamyaham.

(translation)

> I offer honor and respect to Shree Mangala,
> The god of the planet Mars,
> Who was born from the womb of the earth goddess.
> His brilliant effulgence is like that of lightning,
> And he appears as a youth carrying
> A spear in his hand.

<u>Prayers</u>

God is my strength and power:
and he maketh my way perfect.
2 Samuel, 22:33

In God is my salvation and my glory:
the rock of my strength and my refuge is in God.
Psalms, 62:7

They that wait upon the LORD
Shall renew their strength;
They shall mount up with wings as eagles;
They shall run, and not be weary;
And they shall walk, and not faint.
Isaiah, 40:31

<u>*Pujas* and *Yagyas:*</u>

Contact <u>www.puja.net</u> or <u>www.amma.org</u> to arrange *pujas* or *yagyas* .

BALANCING ENERGY SYSTEM 4/MERCURY

ES4/MERCURY Table of Correspondences

SHAPE: Triangle.

WEEKDAY: Wednesday.

DIVINITIES: Mercury, Hermes, Budha, Thoth, Coyote (trickster), Vishnu, Archangel Raphael.

PEOPLE: Maternal uncles, artisans, accountants, educated persons, astrologers, craftspersons, students, tradespersons, clerks, orators, merchants, thieves, secretaries, mathematicians, printers, messengers, delivery-persons, stationers, lawyers, debaters, elementary teachers. Also represents the rational mind (not emotions) and speech.

PARTS OF BODY: Hands, lungs, eyes, ears, fingers, central nervous system, thyroid gland, five senses, the pinky finger.

ANIMALS: Parrots, cats, coyotes, foxes, hyenas, apes, squirrels, weasels, spiders, greyhounds, bees, swallows, locusts, cranes.

PLANTS: Green leaves, plants with seeds in husks or cobs, small plants, wildflowers, walnut trees, filbert trees, elder trees, reeds, fruitless trees, plumerias, plants with clusters of flowers or fruits, plants that feature multiple tiny leaves.

FOODS: Root vegetables and spices, (carrots, parsnips, turnips, potatoes, rutabagas, *etc.*), okra, nectarines, hybridized fruits and vegetables, walnuts, filberts, lungwort, gotu kola, skullcap, passion flowers, chamomile, mints, sage, basil, eucalyptus, thyme, pumpkins, squashes.

PLACES: Businesses (places of trade), libraries, transportation and communication centers, playgrounds, bookstores, fairs, post offices, accounting firms, parks, public assemblies, bowling alleys, tennis courts, places of sports of skill, not violence.

GEMS AND MINERALS: Emerald, peridot, tsavorite garnet, chrome diopside, green tourmaline, natural green jade, brass, quicksilver (Mercury).

GRAINS: Mung beans.

COLORS: Green.

BALANCING ACTIVITIES

Charity and Service — Examples:

On Wednesdays, do one or more of the following activities:

➤ Give wildflowers or green, leafy plants to an ES4/Mercury person or place. You can give these to libraries or bookstores, students, or grade-school teachers, or plant them at the edge of a playground.

➤ Give unsweetened pumpkin in charity to an educated person, craftsperson, accountant, astrologer, student, tradesperson or merchant, secretary, mathematician, lawyer, printer, clerk, elementary teacher, or to a squirrel, coyote or other representative of ES4/Mercury.

➤ Give green colored gifts to the people or animals of ES4/Mercury.

➤ Feed root vegetables (potatoes, parsnips, turnips, carrots) to a cat (one who will eat them), or to your maternal uncle.

➤ Use the ES4/Mercury Table of Correspondences to mix and match your own charity or service.

Candle Ritual — Example:

The following steps comprise an example of a candle ritual. As you become more familiar with the correspondences for ES4/Mercury, you may vary this process to better match your inclinations.

1. Light a green candle (FIRE) at dawn (or whenever you get up) on Wednesday.

2. Tamp out the match in a dish of earth (EARTH).

3. Surround the candle with green leafy plants, wildflowers, green stones, (EARTH), and images (statues or photographs) of ES4/Mercury representatives.

4. Use your breath (AIR) to express appreciation for the archetype of ES4/Mercury, requesting that only the most auspicious of its energies affect your life (ETHER).

5. Repeat a simple ES4/Mercury *mantra* (ETHER).

6. Dampen your fingers (or a stick) with water (WATER) to pinch out the flame.

7. Release your breath and intention to the universe (ETHER).

Fasting and Food Rituals — Examples:

➤ Fast on nine consecutive Wednesdays (with the permission of your medical professional).

➤ On nine consecutive Wednesdays, or for nine consecutive days starting on Wednesday, refrain from eating root vegetables and spices (such as potatoes, carrots, parsnips, turnips, rutabagas, *etc.*), hybridized fruits and vegetables, walnuts, filberts, okra, nectarines, chamomile, mints, sage, basil, eucalyptus, thyme, pumpkins, squash.

➤ Give the above foods to ES4/Mercury people as charity.

➤ Alternately, go out of your way to consume several of these foods on Wednesdays, particularly any that are not a normal part of your diet.

Other Rituals — Examples:

➤ On Wednesdays, use mung beans or green yarn to create the shape of a triangle outside your front door, on your altar, your desk, kitchen workspace, or patio. You can also sing ES4/ Mercury *mantras* while you create this triangle, and fill or surround it with ES4 items.

➤ Place a green, translucent glass filled with water in the sunlight on Wednesday mornings. Drink the water in the evening to ingest ES4/Mercury.

Creative Homage — Examples:

On Wednesdays,

➤ Draw, paint, sculpt or do needlework to create an image of Mercury, Hermes, Budha (not Buddha), Thoth, Coyote or other representatives of trickster archetypes, or Vishnu, or Archangel Raphael.

➤ Create the above picture using "*Mantra* Painting," — writing tiny, curving ES4/Mercury *mantras* or prayers in place of penciled lines and solid blocks of color.

➤ Use shades of green to compose your image.

➤ Sing, or silently say ES4/Mercury *mantras* while you create.

➤ Compose and sing a song honoring Mercury or any of the persons or divine beings associated with ES4/Mercury.

➤ Compose a song or poem for a favorite elementary school teacher and give it to him/her if possible.

Healing Stories — Examples:

On Wednesdays, do one or more of the following activities:

➤ Read stories about Mercury, Hermes, Thoth, Coyote or trickster archetypes, Vishnu, or Archangel Raphael.

➤ Alternatively, write your own stories about the above figures.

➤ Write a story about sneakily clever school-children.

➤ Read "picaresque" style novels (an ancient genre, usually about young men, who wander the world getting into and out of scrapes with the law and having adventures).

> ➢ Read **_Don Quixote_**, watch the musical, **_Man from La Mancha_**, or sing the songs.

Mantras and Prayers:

Select one of the _mantras_ from the list below. While you may repeat these on any day, be <u>sure</u> to do it on Wednesdays. When Sanskrit is available, use Sanskrit. Translations do not carry the same vibrational power.

Seed _Mantras_

- OM Bum   (pronounced as short u –bum)
- OM Aim   (pronounced like the word eye with an "m" at the end: eye-m)

Simple _Mantra_

- OM Bum Budha Namaha.

Budha (Mercury) Gayatri

OM GaJadwajaya Vidmahe
Shuka Hasthaya Dheemahi.
Dhano Budha Prachodayat.

(translation)

Let me meditate on Mercury;
He who has power to grant pleasure.
Let Budha enlighten me.

Other *Mantra*

OM Priyangava Gulikashaym rupena
Pratimambudam Sauyam
Saumya gunopetam
Tam budham pranamamyaham.

(translation)

I give honor to Mercury,
Whose beloved body is dark like the night,
The symbol of intelligence,
And whose qualities are most beautiful.

Prayer

Let the words of my mouth,
And the meditation of my heart,
Be acceptable in thy sight,
O LORD, my strength, and my redeemer.
Psalm 19:14

Pujas and *Yagyas*:

Contact www.puja.net or www.amma.org to arrange *pujas* or *yagyas*.

BALANCING ENERGY SYSTEM 5/JUPITER

ES5/JUPITER Table of Correspondences

SHAPE: Ellipse.

WEEKDAY: Thursday.

DIVINITIES: Brihaspati, Ganesha, Jupiter, Zeus, Thor, Bear
(American Indian), Archangel Zadkiel.

PEOPLE: Children, one's own children, inspired teachers,
gurus, wise or learned persons, counselors,
clergy, judges, legislators, philosophers, money-
lenders, scholars, university students, professors,
lawyers, world travelers. Also represents
knowledge, fortune, religion, spirituality, law.

PARTS OF BODY: Thighs, liver, alimentary canal, pituitary
gland, index finger.

ANIMALS: Elephants, horses, swans, pigeons, sheep, stags,
does, oxen, dragons, mild and gentle animals,
storks, larks, eagles, bees, pheasants, peacocks,
hens, whales.

PLANTS: Yellow flowers, flax, violets, peonies, fig trees,
pear trees, hazelnut trees, beech trees, pine trees,
fruit trees, jasmine, daisies.

FOODS: Chickpeas, fatty foods, sweet flavors, butter,
ghee, cream, gourds, pumpkins, squash, berries,
sugars, dates, honey, olive oil, sweet herbs,
peppermint, spearmint, sweet wines, cloves,
mace, nutmeg, strawberries, balsam, rhubarb,
borage, willow herb, basil, licorice, saffron,
turmeric, dahl, ginseng, astragalus, almonds,
walnuts, cashews, sesame seeds, sesame or
almond oil.

PLACES: Treasuries, universities, monasteries, banks, "official" places (such as courthouses and courtrooms), altars, society balls, charitable institutions, political assemblies, stock and commodity markets, churches, places of oratory.

GEMS AND MINERALS: Yellow sapphire, citrine, yellow topaz, gold.

GRAINS: Chickpeas.

COLORS: Yellow, gold.

BALANCING ACTIVITIES

Charity and Service — Examples:

On Thursdays, do one or more of the following activities:

➤ Give yellow flowers (without thorns) to your children, your father, to inspired teachers, clergy, wise people, university students or professors, or to good attorneys.

➤ Give yellow flowers to universities, monasteries, churches, or charitable institutions.

➤ Give saffron, turmeric, dahl, or gold in charity to a person associated with ES5/Jupiter.

➤ Give daisies to a doe, swan, or sheep.

➤ With the permission of your medical professional, give your children or your father sweet and fatty foods, dates, honey, peppermint, spearmint, basil, licorice, almonds, walnuts, cashews, garbanzo beans (chickpeas) or sesame seeds.

➤ Plant a pear tree at a university, charitable institution, monastery, or church. (Get permission.)

➤ Give ES5/Jupiter foods to charities that help children.

➤ Use the Table of Correspondence to mix and match your own charity or service.

Candle Ritual – Example:

The following steps comprise an example of a candle ritual. As you become more familiar with the correspondences for ES5/Jupiter, you may vary this process to better match your inclinations.

1. Light a yellow candle (FIRE) at dawn (or whenever you get up) on Thursday.

2. Tamp out the match in a dish of earth (EARTH).

3. Surround the candle with yellow thorn-less flowers, yellow stones, (EARTH), and images (statues or photographs) of Jupiter representatives, including your father, your guru or great spiritual masters. Ganesha is one of the Indian deities associated with ES5/Jupiter, so a statue of Ganesha or of an elephant is very appropriate.

4. Use your breath (AIR) to express appreciation for the energy of ES5/Jupiter, requesting that only the most auspicious of its energies affect your life (ETHER).

5. Repeat an ES5/Jupiter *mantra* (ETHER).

6. Dampen your fingers (or a stick) with water (WATER) to pinch out the flame.

7. Release your breath and intention to the universe (ETHER).

Fasting and Food Rituals — Examples:

> Fast on nine consecutive Thursdays (with the permission of your medical advisor).

> For nine consecutive Thursdays, or for nine consecutive days, starting on Thursday, refrain from eating sweet or fatty foods, butter, gourds, pumpkins, squash, berries, any sweet foods or sweeteners, sweet wines, cloves, nutmeg, straw-berries, rhubarb, basil, licorice, dahl, ginseng, almonds, walnuts, cashews, sesame seeds or other foods related to ES5/Jupiter.

> Give the above foods to ES5/Jupiter people as charity.

> Alternately, go out of your way to consume several of these foods on Thursday, particularly those foods that are not a part of your normal diet.

Other Rituals — Examples:

On Thursdays, do one or more of the following activities:

> Use chickpeas (garbanzo beans), or yellow yarn to create the shape of an ellipse outside your front door, on your altar, dining table, outside patio or library desk.

> In the morning, place a yellow, translucent glass filled with water in the sunlight. Drink the water in the evening to ingest ES5/Jupiter (light through the yellow glass).

Creative Homage — Examples:

➢ On Thursday, draw, paint, sculpt, or create needlework to make an image of Ganesha, Jupiter, Brihaspati, Zeus, Thor, Bear (American Indian) or of ES5/Jupiter people such as Mahatma Gandhi, Martin Luther King, or great teachers, lawmakers, or spiritual advisors in your own life.

➢ Create an image of your own children, or your father or grandfather using these techniques.

➢ Create the above picture using *"Mantra Painting,"* -- writing tiny, curving ES5/Jupiter *mantras* or prayers instead of penciled lines and solid blocks of color.

➢ Use yellow and gold colors to create your image.

➢ Sing, or silently say ES5/Jupiter *mantras* or prayers while you work.

➢ Compose and sing a song honoring any of the representatives of the ES5/Jupiter archetype.

Healing Stories — Examples:

On Thursdays, do one or more of the following activities:

➢ Read stories about Jupiter, Zeus, Brihaspati, Ganesha, Mahatma Gandhi, or great spiritual masters.

➢ Or read **The Ugly Duckling** by Hans Christian Anderson.

➢ Or read stories about **Babar, The Elephant**, by Jean de Brunhoff, or Dr. Seuss stories about Horton the Elephant (**Horton Hatches the Egg, Horton Hears a Who**).

➢ Or write your own stories about these figures, about your children, your father, or your grandfather, or about great and generous elephants.

168

> ➢ Create and produce puppet plays about elephants, swans, horses, stags, peacocks, whales, or dragons.

> ➢ Read (or write) histories about great universities, monasteries, churches, society balls, or charitable institutions.

Mantras and Prayers:

Select one of the *mantras* or prayers from the list below. While you may repeat these on any day, be sure to do it on Thursday. When Sanskrit is available, use Sanskrit. Translations do not carry the same vibrational power.

Seed *Mantras*

- OM Shrim
- OM Brahm

Simple *Mantras*

- OM Gum Ganapatayei Namaha. (most frequently used)

- OM Bum Brihaspataye Namaha.
- OM Gurave Namaha

Ganesha *Mantra*

OM Gananan-tva
Ganapatiqum havamahey
Kavin Kavinam
Upama Shravastamam
Jyesthara-jam Brahmanam
Brahmana spata Anas Srinvan
Nutibhissi dasadanam
Sri Maha-ganapataye Namaha.

(translation)

Come and sit near us and hear our prayer
To remove all Obstacles to happiness,
success, wisdom, and abundance.

Guru (Jupiter) Gayatri

OM Vrisha Bhadwajaya Vidmahe
Ghrini Hasthaya Dheemahi
Dhano Guru Prachodayat.

(translation)

Let me meditate on Jupiter:
He who has power to get things done.
Let Guru enlighten me.

Other *Mantra*

Deva Namcha Rishinamcha gurum
Kanchana Sannibham budchee-bhutam
Tri-lokesham tam namam, Brihaspatim.

(translation)

I pray to Jupiter (Guru)
The teacher of Gods and Rishis,
Intellect incarnate,
Lord of the three worlds.

Mrityunjaya *Mantra*

If Jupiter is under-active or malefic, use this *mantra*.

OM, Tryumbakam yayamahe,
Shugandhim pushti Vardhanam.
Urdvaru Kamiva Bandhanan.
Mrityor, Mukshiya mam ritad.

(translation)

170

We meditate on Shiva,
The three-eyed one of sweet fragrance,
Who expands spiritual growth.
Like the fully-ripened fruit drops from its stem
May I be free from the bondage of death
And attachment in life,
But not from immortality.

The Lord's Prayer

Our Father, which art in heaven,
Hallowed be thy name.
Thy kingdom come, thy will be done,
On earth as it is in heaven.
Give us this day our daily bread,
And forgive us our trespasses,
As we forgive those who trespass against us.
Lead us not into temptation,
But deliver us from evil.
For Thine is the kingdom, the power,
And the glory, forever.
Amen.

Doxology

Praise God from whom all blessings flow.
Praise Him all creatures here below.
Praise Him above, ye heavenly host.
Praise Father, Son, and Holy Ghost.
Amen.

Pujas and *Yagyas*:

Contact www.puja.net or www.amma.org to arrange *pujas* or *yagyas*.

171

BALANCING ENERGY SYSTEM 6/VENUS

ES5/VENUS Table of Correspondences

SHAPE: Octagon.

WEEKDAY: Friday.

DIVINITIES: Venus, Aphrodite, Sukra, Lakshmi, Parvati, Saraswati, Kuculcan (Mayan), Quetzalquatl (Aztec), Indrani, Innana, Rhada and Krishna, Astarte, Archangel Anael.

PEOPLE: Marriage partner, actors, performers, artists, persons dealing with beauty (beauticians, interior decorators, *etc.*) musicians, designers, restaurateurs, diplomats, people involved with fashion and clothing, perfumers, cosmeticians, jewelry designers, pre-pubescent girls. Also desires and yearnings, marriage.

PARTS OF BODY: Throat, kidneys, thymus gland, sense of touch, ovaries, the large muscle at the base of the thumb.

ANIMALS: Peacocks, parrots, cows, buffaloes, horses and large animals, the hart, calves, doves, thrushes, wrens, pelicans, partridges, swans, swallows, dolphins.

PLANTS: White flowers, blossoming trees, fragrant flowers, white lotus, cotton, silk, sandalwood, garden flowers, creepers and vines, roses, jasmine, lilies, irises, myrtle, sweet herbs, daffodils, white sycamores, wild ash trees, turpentine tree, olive tree, camphor.

FOODS: Fancy and exotic fruits and vegetables, pomegranates, gooseberries, sugars, refined sweeteners, candies and sweet foods, liqueurs, processed but essential foods, saffron, tonics, aloe gel, red raspberries, sweet apples, figs, sweet oranges, walnuts, almonds, millet, valerian, thyme, laudanum, coriander, wheat flour, peaches, apricots, plums, sour flavors, ghee.

PLACES: Theaters, restaurants, fancy automobiles, places of amusement, places of beauty and art, fine clothing stores, bedrooms, brothels, art galleries, music halls or places of musical performances, dance halls or places where people dance, opera and symphony auditoriums, formal gardens, bridal chambers, dancing schools.

GEMS AND MINERALS: Diamond, white sapphire, white topaz, quartz, silver, copper.

GRAINS: Lima beans, millet.

COLORS: Rainbow colors, bright pastel colors (multi-colored), white.

BALANCING ACTIVITIES

Charity and Service — Examples:

On Fridays, do one or more of the following activities:

➤ Give white flowers or pastel-colored flowers with a pleasing scent to young women, musicians, artists, actors, designers, decorators, or other ES6/Venus divinities or personages. For example, give a white flower to a beautician, art gallery owner, or a young girl every Friday.

➤ Give a part of your meal to cows.

➤ Give away clear quartz crystals, ghee, camphor, to ES6/Venus people or places.

> Take up the maintenance of a poor section of the public, especially in service to women.

> Offer poor women (women who can't afford it) beauty treatments, cosmetics, or give jewelry. (You could work with a salon to make this offer available.)

> On at least nine consecutive Fridays, give ES6/ Venus objects to ES6/Venus related persons, animals, or places.

> Use the ES6/Venus Table of Correspondences to mix and match your own charity or service.

Candle Ritual — Example:

The following steps comprise an example of a candle ritual. As you become more familiar with the correspondences for ES1/Venus you may vary this process to better match your inclinations.

1. Light a white, scented candle, (FIRE), at dawn (or whenever you get up) on Friday.

2. Tamp out the match in a dish of earth (EARTH).

3. Surround the candle with white scented flowers, clear stones or clear crystals EARTH), and rock candy. Add images (statues or photographs) of Venus, Aphrodite, Sukra, Lakshmi, Parvati, Kuculcan (Mayan), Quetzalquatl, Saraswati, Indrani, Rhada and Krishna, Astarte, Innana, or of famous and beautiful actors, performers, artists, designers, or other representatives of ES6/Venus archetypes. You can also include art images, and scenes and people of great beauty.

4. Invoke the energy of ES6/Venus with a side-ways glance at your altar. (The "sideways glance" is

characteristic of this ES. It is nearly impossible to do without at least a hint of flirtation!) (ETHER)

5. Use your breath (AIR) to express appreciation for ES6/Venus principles, requesting that only the most auspicious of its influences affect your life (ETHER).

6. Repeat a simple ES6/Venus *mantra* (ETHER).

7. Dampen your fingers (or a stick) with water (WA-TER) to pinch out the flame.

8. Release your breath and intention to the universe (ETHER).

Fasting and Food Rituals — Examples:

➢ Fast on nine consecutive Fridays (with the permission of your medical advisor).

➢ On nine consecutive Fridays, or on nine consecutive days starting on Friday, refrain from eating fancy or exotic fruits and vegetables, pomegranates, sugar or refined sweeteners, candy and sweet foods, liqueurs, processed essential foods, raspberries, sweet apples, figs, sweet oranges, walnuts, almonds, valerian, thyme, coriander, wheat flour, peaches, apricots, plums, ghee, or other ES6/Venus foods.

➢ Give the above foods to ES6/Venus people as charity.

➢ Alternately, go out of your way to consume several of these foods on Fridays, particularly those foods that are NOT a normal part of your diet.

Other Rituals — Examples:

On Fridays, do one or more of the following activities:

➤ Place a clear, crystal glass filled with water in the sunlight on Friday mornings. Drink the water in the evening to ingest ES6/Venus influences (via the light through the crystal glass).

➤ Using millet or lima beans, or using pastel green silk or pastel sparkly yarn, create the shape of an octagon outside of the front door of your home, or on your desk, sidewalk, or patio. You can also repeat ES6/Venus *mantras* while you create the octagon, and/or add ES6 items to the inside or outside of your octagon.

Creative Homage — Examples:

➤ Starting on Fridays, draw, paint, sculpt, or create needlework to make an image of Venus, Aphrodite, Sukra, Lakshmi, Parvati, Saraswati, Kuculcan, Quetzalquatl, Indrani, Rhada and Krishna, Astarte, beautiful or handsome actors you admire, or other ES6/Venus divinities or personages who represent beauty and desire.

➤ You can also create art about doves, swans, swallows, dolphins, blossoming trees, or white lotus flowers.

➤ Create these pictures using *"Mantra* Painting," — writing tiny, curving ES6/ Venus *mantras* in place of penciled lines and solid blocks of color.

➤ Use whites, pastel colors, and sparkles -- like glitter or sparkly media -- to create your images.

➤ On Fridays, use silk threads, yarn or cloth to create beautiful images or to design clothing for anyone representing an ES6/Venus persons or divinities.

➢ Sing or silently say ES6/Venus *mantras* while you work.

➢ Compose and sing a song to love in any of its forms.

Healing Stories — Examples:

On Fridays, do one or more of the following activities:

➢ Read about Venus, Aphrodite, Sukra, Lakshmi, Parvati, Saraswati, Kuculcan, Indrani, Rhada and Krishna, Astarte, or read biographies of great artists, great beauties, film stars, designers, or decorators.

➢ Or write your own stories about these figures.

➢ Write your own love story: biographical or fictional.

➢ Read or write stories about peacocks, parrots, cows, horses (read **_The Horse Whisperer_** by Nicholas Evans or watch the movie, or read **_Black Beauty_** by Anna Sewell), harts, calves, doves, wrens, pelicans, swans, swallows, dolphins. Watch the movie **_Monsoon Wedding_**.

Mantras and Prayers:

Select one of the *mantras* from the list below. While you can repeat these *mantras* on any day, be sure to do it on Fridays. When Sanskrit is available, use Sanskrit. Translations do not carry the same vibrational power.

Seed *Mantras*

- OM Shreem
- OM Hreem
- OM Shum

Simple *Mantras*

- OM Shum Shukraya Namaha.

- OM Shreem Lakshmiaiya Namaha.

Sukra (Venus) Gayatri

OM Ashwadhwa jaya Vidmahe
Dhanur hastaya Dheemahi
Dhano Sukra, Prachodayat.

(translation)

Let me meditate on Venus;
He who has a bow in his hand
And let Sukra enlighten me.

Lakshmi *Mantra*

OM harem kale ayes
Kamala, kamalah-ee-eh,
Praseedup praseeda
Sahala saubagyam Dehi Dehi
OM shreem mahalakshmi namo Namaha.

(translation)

(General *mantra* for love and abundance.)

Other *Mantra*

Heema-Kunda mrinaLabham
Daityanam Paranam gurum
Sarva Shastra pravaKtaram
Bhargavam pranamamyahnam.

(translation)

I offer my obeisance to
the descendent of Bhrigu Muni, *(i.e.,* Venus),
Whose complexion is white like a pond
Covered with ice.

He is the supreme spiritual master
of the demoniac enemies of the demigods,
In addition, has spoken to them all the revealed scriptures.

<u>Native American Prayer:</u>

Oh Great Spirit
Whose voice I hear in the winds
And whose breath gives life to all the world,
Hear me!
I am small and weak,
I need your strength and wisdom.

Let me walk in beauty, and make my eyes
Ever behold the red and purple sunset.

Make my hands respect the things you have made
And my ears sharp to hear your voice.

Make me wise so that I may understand
The things you have taught my people.

Let me learn the lessons you have hidden
In every leaf and rock.

I seek strength, not to be greater than my brother,
But to fight my greatest enemy — myself.

Make me always ready to come to you
With clean hands and straight eyes.

So when life fades, as the fading sunset,
My spirit may come to you without shame.
Sioux Indian Prayer

Pujas and *Yagya*:

Contact www.puja.net or www.amma.org to arrange
pujas or *yagyas*.

BALANCING ENERGY SYSTEM 7/SATURN

ES7/SATURN Table of Correspondences

SHAPE: Square window with four panes.

WEEKDAY: Saturday.

DIVINITIES: Shiva (the "destroyer" principle of the Hindu
             trinity), Yama (god of death), Kali (the fierce
             mother), Osiris (the Egyptian god of death and the
             underworld), Saturn, Kronos, Sani, Archangel
             Cassiel, Spirits of Ancestors, Saint Dismas, Saint
             Benedict Joseph Labre.

PEOPLE: Servants, old people, grandfathers, people who
            deal with old or dead things (historians,
            morticians, geriatric aid workers, leather-workers,
            archaeologists), people who deal with earth
            products (miners, drillers, gemologists, stone-
            carvers, *etc.*), laborers, monks, renunciates,
            isolated people, vagrants, prisoners, beggars, the
            homeless, plumbers, chimney sweeps.

PARTS OF BODY: Skin, bones, hair, teeth, fingernails and
            toenails, second finger of hand (not counting
            thumb).

ANIMALS: Crows, vultures, donkeys, turtles/tortoises,
            wolves, crocodiles, scorpions, toads, snakes,
            creeping creatures, creatures that live or breed in
            ruins, putrefaction and decay; bats, owls.

PLANTS: Violets, dead wood, purple flowers, thorny wood,
            bearsfoot, ferns, starwort, wolfbane, hemlock,
            clover, alfalfa, henbane, mandrake, poppies,
            angelica, rue, willow trees, yew trees, cypress
            trees, pine trees, hemp.

FOODS: Junk foods, pickled foods, burdock, sage, spinach, cumin, capers, parsnips, hard-to-digest foods, peas, soybeans, dark rye bread, dark brown or black foods.

PLACES: Dirty or old places, slums, cemeteries, graveyards, prisons, dark woods, deserts, obscure valleys, caves or dens, holes, ruined buildings, coalmines, stinking places.

GEMS AND MINERALS: Blue sapphire, lapis lazuli, black and ugly stones, lead, iron, lodestone (natural magnets).

GRAINS: Sesame seeds, rye.

COLORS: Dark blue, dark purple, black, gray, brown.

BALANCING ACTIVITIES

Before doing anything else for ES7/Saturn, make sure you've followed all the RULES of the society you belong to. Pay any taxes or parking tickets, arrive to work on time and don't leave early, follow all the rules society imposes. Saturn respects rules and will clobber you when you have not followed them. Not following these rules creates a malefic ES7/Saturn, and you definitely don't want that.

Charity and Service — Examples:

On Saturdays, do one or more of the following activities:

➢ Give purple flowers (violets, irises, *etc.*) to shut-ins, the elderly, someone who is hospitalized or chronically ill.

➢ Give dark colored food (coffee, dark chocolate, rye bread, sunflower seeds, black beans, blue corn chips, *etc.*) to a homeless person.

➢ Feed crows, pigeons, starlings, grackles, or other "nuisance birds" sunflower seeds, dark rye bread or other dark colored foods.

➢ Alternately, give ES7/Saturn items to a leather worker, historian, mortician, geriatric worker, archaeologist, miner, stonecarver, monk or renunciate.

➢ Feed small balls of wheat flour to fish.

➢ Volunteer in a homeless shelter, hospital or prison.

➢ Clean trash and weeds from a vacant lot.

➢ Tidy a graveyard, clearing weeds and trash and mowing the lawn where appropriate. Repairing broken or tilted gravestones is also useful, but gain permission first.

➢ Take trash to a recycling center.

➢ Give attractive driftwood, or art made from trash, or ferns, clover, poppies, spinach, or capers to an ES7/Saturn archetype.

➢ Use sesame or rye seeds, or use black yarn to create a square 'window' shape with a cross in it (to look like a window with four panes) on your altar, your front porch, near the trashcans, or on the back step of your house.

> ➢ Use the ES7/Saturn Table of Correspondences to mix and match your own charity or service.

> ➢ <u>NOTE</u>: With ES7, many of the items are not generally considered desirable. When offering an ES7 item to someone or some place, be reasonably certain it is something that won't insult them. For example, don't give trash to homeless people.

<u>Candle Ritual</u> — Example:

The following steps comprise an example of a candle ritual. As you become more familiar with the correspondences for ES7/Saturn, you may vary this process to better match your inclinations.

1. Light a dark blue or black candle (FIRE) at dawn (or whenever you get up) on Saturday.

2. Tamp out the match in a dish of earth (EARTH).

3. Surround the candle with dead or thorny branches, blue or black stones (EARTH) and images (statues or photographs) of Shiva, Yama, Kali, Osiris, Saturn, Kronos, Sani, Archangel Cassiel, Spirits of Ancestors, Saint Dismas, Saint Benedict Joseph Labre (who worked with lepers). You could also include images of grandfathers, great historians, archaeologists, monks.

4. Use your breath (AIR) to express appreciation for the enduring qualities of ES7/Saturn, requesting that only the most auspicious of its potentials affect your life (ETHER).

5. Repeat a simple ES7/Saturn *mantra* or prayer. (ETHER)

6. Use a drop of water to put out the flame (WATER).

7. Release your breath and intention to the universe (ETHER).

Fasting and Food Rituals — Examples:

➤ Fast on nine consecutive Saturdays (with the permission of your medical professional).

➤ On nine consecutive Saturdays, or on nine consecutive days starting on Saturday, refrain from eating junk foods, pickled foods, sage, spinach, cumin, capers, parsnips, hard-to-digest foods, soybeans, dark rye bread, dark brown or black foods, coffee, sunflower seeds, dark chocolate, or any of the foods related to ES7/Saturn.

➤ Give the above foods to ES7/Saturn people as charity.

➤ Alternately, go out of your way to consume several of these foods on Saturdays, particularly those foods that are NOT a normal part of your diet.

➤ On Saturdays, clean out your refrigerator of all old foods, eating from those that are still good and discarding the rest.

Other Rituals — Examples:

➤ On Saturday morning, fill a translucent, cobalt blue glass with water and place it where it receives sunlight during the day. Drink the water in the evening to strengthen ES7/Saturn. CAUTION: Do this only if you are trying to increase the good qualities of ES7. If you are suffering from its bad qualities this is not a safe activity. If you experience any bad qualities of Saturn after doing this, stop immediately.

➤ Using sesame seeds or rye seeds, draw a square "four-window-pane" shape on your front porch, patio, mud-room floor, or near your trash cans on Saturdays. Sing ES7/Saturn mantras as you work.

Creative Homage — Examples:

➤ On Saturdays, draw, paint, dance, sculpt, or create music utilizing the colors, divinities, persons, principles, *mantras*, and prayers of ES7/Saturn.

➤ Create images of Shiva, Yama, Kali, Osiris, Saturn, Kronos, Sani, Archangel Cassiel, Spirits of Ancestors, Saint Dismas, Saint Benedict Joseph Labre. You could also create images of your grandfathers, of great historians, archaeologists, or monks.

➤ Create the above picture using *"Mantra* Painting," -- writing tiny, curving ES7/Saturn *mantras* or prayers in place of penciled lines and solid blocks of color.

➤ Use dark blues, dark purples, indigo, black, and dark grays to create your image.

➤ Sing or silently say ES7/Saturn prayers or *mantras* while you work.

➤ Compose and sing a song honoring any of the divine or archetypal beings associated with ES7/Saturn.

➤ Sing the blues.

Healing Stories — Examples:

On Saturdays, do one or more of the following activities:

> Read or write stories or biographies of any of the deities or personages related to ES7/Saturn or any of its representatives.

> Read Robert Svoboda's ***The Greatness of Saturn***, the Biblical ***Book of Job,*** or Archibald MacLeish's Pulitzer and Tony-winning play, ***J.B***.

> Write your own stories about people who have endured difficulties and succeeded, or those who have worked with extraordinary diligence to reach their goals.

> Create and produce puppet plays about donkeys, turtles, wolves, crocodiles, scorpions, snakes, bats, owls, or other ES7 animals.

> Listen to great requiem masses, like Mozart's ***Requiem***, or Gabriel Faure's ***Requiem***. (Use caution here—you may get too much strengthening of Saturn which can be difficult. Best if you also move your body or sing with the music to allow the energy to move through you instead of getting stuck.)

> Write your own song and sing the blues.

> Compose and sing a song honoring any of the divine or archetypal beings associated with ES7/Saturn.

Mantras and Prayers:

Select one or more of the *mantras* below. When Sanskrit is available, use Sanskrit. Translations do not carry the same vibrational power. While you may repeat the *mantras* on any day, be <u>sure</u> to do it on Saturdays.

Seed *Mantras*

- Kleem

- OM Sham (pronounced like "chum")

- OM Shanti Shanti

Simple *Mantras*

- OM Sri Shanaischaraya Namaha.   *(before age 30)*

- OM Sri Shanaischwaraya Swaha.   *(after age 30)*

- OM Namah Shivaya.   *(most frequently used)*

Mrityunjaya *Mantra*

OM, Tryumbakam yayamahe
Shugandhim pushti Vardhanam
Urdvaru Kamiva Bandhanan
Mrityor, Mukshiya Mam ritad.

(translation)

We meditate on Shiva,
The three-eyed one of sweet fragrance,
Who expands spiritual growth.
Like the fully-ripened fruit drops from its stem,
May I be free from the bondage of death
And attachment in life,
But not from immortality.

187

Sani (Saturn) Gayatri *Mantra*

OM Sanaischaraya Vidmahe,
Sooryaputraya Dheemahi,
Dhano manda Prachodayat.

(translation)

I bow down to slow-moving Saturn,
Whose complexion is dark blue like nilanjana ointment.
The elder brother of Lord Yamaraj,
He is born from the Sun god and his wife Chaya.

Other *Mantra*

Nilanjana samabhasam
Ravi putram yamagrajam
Chaya martanda sambhutam
tam namami sanais charam.

(translation)

I bow to lord Shani, who is black in color
And son of the Sun; who was born to Chaya
And brother of Yama
And who moves very slowly.

The 23rd Psalm

The Lord is My Shepherd, I shall not want.
He maketh me to lie down in green pastures,
He leadeth me beside the still waters,
He restoreth my Soul.
He leadeth me in the paths of righteousness
for His Name's sake.
Yea, though I walk through the Valley of the
Shadow of Death,
I will fear no evil, for Thou art with me.

Thy rod and thy staff they comfort me.
Thou preparest a table before me
in the presence of mine enemies.
Thou anointest my head with oil; my cup runneth over.
Surely goodness and mercy will follow me
All the days of my life
And I will dwell in the house of the Lord forever.
Amen.

Pujas and *Yagyas*:

Contact www.puja.net or www.amma.org to arrange *pujas* or *yagyas*.

10. ACTIVITIES FOR BALANCING <u>SUBTLE</u> ENERGY SYSTEMS

Energy System 8/Rahu, (the Moon's North Node) and Energy System 9/Ketu (the Moon's South Node) are quite different from the material Energy Systems. In astronomical terms, the nodes of the Moon are not physical bodies at all. They are mathematical points where the Sun and Moon cross over each other at solar and lunar eclipses, and the "movement" of these points between eclipses is calculated carefully. Even though they aren't physical bodies, their energy is buried deep in our species' subconscious. While they are non-physical points, and therefore "subtle" energy sources, their effects are anything but subtle.

Eclipses were important in every cultural tradition, and were generally connected with some version of the world gone awry. In western traditions they were associated with the deaths of leaders.

In Egypt, eclipses represented the power of Isis (symbolized by the Moon) over the Sun itself. In the mythologies, Isis poisoned the Sun, creating the Sun's near-death in an eclipse.

She promised an antidote to the poison only if the Sun revealed to her the secrets of creation. Only then did she end the eclipse.

In all traditions, the Nodes are considered to be parts of a Snake or Dragon (archetypally the same symbol), and are demons who can swallow the Sun and the Moon (the eclipses). What happens when the light disappears? If the Sun and Moon are vanquished, we are left in darkness, both literally and spiritually. Therefore, Energy Systems 8 and 9 contain an uneasy and dangerous set of associations.

The East Indian mythology about the Moon's nodes tells us a fascinating story about how our world was created. That story also helps us better understand the symbolism for Energy Systems 8 and 9, and therefore helps us understand ourselves.

In Hindu mythology, the Nodes were created right after the beginning of our world. The gods and demons got together to churn the great ocean of milk — the chaos and life-giving potential of the great void — to create this incarnation of the world. From the void come the lands and oceans, over which gods and demons still fight. Also from the void come gemstones and the nectar of immortality. The gods and demons agreed that the gods would take the nectar and the demons would take the gems. Naga, the great snake, offered his body as the rope to wrap around Mount Meeru, so that the deities could, by pulling on his body, turn the crank to churn the ocean of milk.

When the work was complete, the gods gathered around their nectar of immortality and began their celebration. The demons gathered all the jewels and gloated. Naga the snake, tired by this time, looked around, realized he could use some of that nectar, and joined the gods. He stepped forward and took a sip of nectar when Vishnu, the creator god, saw him and said, *"STOP! You are no god and cannot have this boon!"* And immediately Vishnu took his discus and chopped off Naga's head.

However, Naga had already taken a sip, and was already immortal. His immortal head became Rahu. Rahu has neither body nor digestive system, so he is always hungry for more of everything, but nothing he finds can satisfy or fill him. Without a stomach, the minute food passes his throat it is gone. Naga's other immortal part—the rest of his body— became Ketu. Ketu has the snake's heart and the digestive and elimination systems. Ketu cannot obtain any new sustenance because he has no mouth. His only option is to derive every last bit of nourishment from prior experiences, and eliminate everything toxic or unneeded.

ES8/Rahu energies are obsessive but not necessarily productive. They are associated with a search for novelty, be it new experiences, new acquisitions, or new knowledge. Some people consider it a point of growth -- although the new experiences gained here probably cannot be truly understood in this lifetime: they may enter the head, but they don't enter the heart and cannot be absorbed by the stomach or the "gut."

On the other hand, ES9/Ketu contains the heart, digestive and elimination systems, and is unable to gain anything new. For this reason ES9/Ketu often relates to heart-felt inner contemplation, isolation, learning how to make do with what we have, letting go of what doesn't serve us, and sometimes getting lost in our own inner processes.

BALANCING ENERGY SYSTEM 8/RAHU – MOON'S NORTH NODE

ES8/RAHU Table of Correspondences

SHAPE:	A straight line.
WEEKDAY:	Saturday.
DIVINITIES:	The ES7/Saturn list, plus Rahu and the Kundalini serpent.
PEOPLE:	The ES7/Saturn list, plus eccentrics, foreigners, oddballs, unconventional people, paternal grandfathers.
PARTS OF BODY:	Doesn't apply. Not a physical energy system.
ANIMALS:	The ES7/Saturn list, plus gulls, snakes, poisonous insects, crawling reptiles.
PLANTS:	The ES7/Saturn list, plus cinnamon trees, mustard.
FOODS:	The ES7/Saturn list, plus cinnamon, mustard.
PLACES:	The ES7/Saturn list.
GEMS AND MINERALS:	Hessonite garnet (cinnamon stone), orange zircon, spessartite garnet, mandarin garnet and orange garnet.
GRAINS:	Barley.
COLORS:	Dark reddish brown, dark honey color, black, brown.

BALANCING ACTIVITIES

Charity and Service — Examples:

On Saturdays, do one or more of the following activities:

> ➤ Give your time to elderly and shut-in people.

> ➤ Give part of your own meal to crows, blue jays, or other loud, noisy birds.

> ➤ Give dark red or dark orange flowers to old or shut-in people.

> ➤ Give dark colored foods to eccentrics, foreigners, or to your paternal grandfather.

> ➤ Wash barley with milk and throw it in running water.

> ➤ Throw coconut in a river (fresh moving water).

> ➤ Give mustard as charity to a sweeper, janitor, or housecleaner.

> ➤ Use the ES8/Rahu Table of Correspondences to mix and match your own charity or service.

Candle Ritual — Example:

The following steps comprise an example of a candle ritual. As you become more familiar with the correspondences for ES8/Rahu you may vary this process to better match your inclinations.

1. At dawn on Saturday (or whenever you wake up), light a dark red-orange candle (FIRE).

2. Tamp out the match in a dish of earth (EARTH).

3. Surround the candle with dead or thorny branches, red-brown stones (EARTH), and images (statues or photographs) of snakes, scorpions, eccentric people, or even your paternal grandfather.

195

4. Use your breath (AIR) to express appreciation for the ES8/Rahu, requesting that only the most auspicious of its energies affect your life. (ETHER)

5. Repeat a simple ES8 *mantra* or prayer (ETHER).

6. Dampen your fingers (or a stick) with water (WATER) to pinch out the flame.

7. Release your breath and intention to the universe (ETHER).

Fasting and Food Rituals — Examples:

➢ Fast on nine consecutive Saturdays (with the permission of your medical advisor).

➢ For nine consecutive Saturdays, or for nine days beginning on Saturday, refrain from eating cinnamon, mustard, junk foods, coffee, chocolate, rye breads or other dark-colored foods.

➢ Give the above foods to an eccentric person, streetperson, an elderly person, a chronically ill person, or a shut-in on Saturdays.

➢ Alternately, on Saturdays, go out of your way to consume some of these foods, particularly those that are NOT a part of your regular diet.

Other Rituals — Examples:

➢ Using mustard seeds or ground mustard, draw a straight line on the ground in front of your door, patio, altar, hearth, or kitchen counter on Saturdays. You may also repeat ES8/Rahu *mantras* or prayers and add ES8 items around the line.

➢ Place a translucent, oxblood-red glass filled with water in the sunlight on Saturday mornings. Drink the water in the evening to ingest ES8/Rahu through the light of the colored glass. CAUTION: Do not do this activity if you are afflicted by ES8 problems. This is only for enhancing ES8 qualities. Stop if you begin to see problems.

Creative Homage — Examples:

On Saturdays,

➢ Draw, paint, sculpt, or create needlework to make an image of Rahu, eclipses, snakes, Shiva, Yama, or your own paternal grandfather, or other images representing ES8.

➢ Create the above picture using "*Mantra* Painting," – writing tiny, curving ES8/Rahu *mantras* in place of penciled lines and solid blocks of color.

➢ Use ox-blood reds, dark honey (or iced tea) colors, and browns to create your image.

➢ Sing or silently say ES8/Rahu *mantras* while you work.

➢ Lay the foundation for a new building, or build a fence.

➢ Compose and sing a song honoring any of the correspondences associated with ES8.

Healing Stories — Examples:

On Saturdays, do one or more of the following activities:

> ➤ Read stories or biographies about Shiva, Yama, or about people who are known for eccentricities.

> ➤ Or write your own stories about the above figures or about your paternal grandfather.

> ➤ Create and produce puppet plays about reptiles, poisons, or other representatives of ES8/Rahu.

Mantras and Prayers:

Select one of the *mantras* from the list below. When Sanskrit is available, use Sanskrit. Translations do not carry the same vibrational power. While you may recite the *mantras* on any day, be <u>sure</u> to do it on Saturdays.

Seed *Mantras*

- OM raam rahve namah.

- OM bhraam bhreem bhraum sah rahave namah.

Simple *Mantra*

OM kreem hum hum
tham tham kadharine rahve
ramhreem shreem mem swaha.

Rahu Gayatri *Mantra*

OM Naakadhwa jaaya Vidmahe
Padma hastaaya Dheemahi
Dhano Rahu, Prachodayat.

(translation)

Let me meditate on Rahu,
He who has a lotus in his hand.
Let Rahu enlighten me.

Mrityunjaya *Mantra*

OM, Tryumbakam yayamahe,
Shugandhim pushti Vardhanam.
Urdvaru Kamiva Bandhanan.
Mrityor, Mukshiya mam ritad.

(translation)

We meditate on Shiva,
The three-eyed one of sweet fragrance,
Who expands spiritual growth.
Like the fully-ripened fruit drops from its stem
May I be free from the bondage of death
And attachment in life,
But not from immortality.

Other *Mantra*

OM Arda-kayam maha-viryam
Chandra ditya veemar-danam
Seeng-hee-ka garba sambootam
Tam rahum prana-mam mya-ham.

(translation)

I offer my respect to Rahu,
Born from the womb of Simhika,
Who has only half a body yet possesses great power,
Being able to subdue the Sun and the Moon.

Pujas and *Yagyas:*

Contact www.puja.net or www.amma.org to arrange
pujas or *yagyas.*

BALANCING ENERGY SYSTEM 9/KETU — MOON'S SOUTH NODE

ES9/KETU Table of Correspondences

SHAPE: A flag on a pole.

WEEKDAY: Saturday.

DIVINITIES: The ES7/Saturn list, plus Ketu and the Kundalini serpent.

PEOPLE: The ES7/Saturn list, plus fisher people, *saddhus*.

PARTS OF BODY: Doesn't apply. Not a physical energy system.

ANIMALS: The ES7/Saturn list, plus owls, snakes, amphibians.

PLANTS: The ES7/Saturn list, plus thorny plants, red flowers.

FOODS: The ES7/Saturn list.

PLACES: The ES7/Saturn list, plus monasteries, temples, ashrams, retreat centers.

GEMS AND MINERALS: Cats-eye, tigers-eye, chrysoberyl, lead, earth.

GRAINS: Red lentils, sesame seeds.

COLORS: Yellowish brown.

BALANCING ACTIVITIES

Charity and Services — Examples:

On Saturdays, do one or more of the following activities:

> ➤ Give orange flowers to old or shut-in people.

> ➤ Feed dogs who are not your pet, or take gifts of dog-food to animal shelters.

> ➤ Donate a blanket to a temple or ashram.

> ➤ Give red lentils or sesame seeds to a retreat center or to a monk.

> ➤ Offer junk food or a dark colored food to a homeless person or to fishermen.

> ➤ Use the ES9/Ketu Table of Correspondences to mix and match your own charity or service.

Candle Ritual — Example:

The following steps comprise an example of a candle ritual. As you become more familiar with the correspondences for ES9/Ketu you may vary this process to better match your inclinations.

1. At dawn on Saturday (or whenever you wake up), light an orange candle (FIRE).

2. Tamp out the match in a dish of earth (EARTH).

3. Surround the candle with branches from thorny plants, yellow-brown stones (EARTH), and images (statues or photographs) of turtles or other amphibians, *saddhus* (begging monks), or temples.

4. Use your breath (AIR) to express appreciation for ES9/Ketu, requesting that only the most auspicious of its energies affect your life (ETHER).

5. Sing or silently repeat a simple ES9/Ketu *mantra* (ETHER).

6. Use a drop of water on your fingertips or a stick to pinch out the flame (WATER).

7. Release your breath and intention to the universe (ETHER).

Fasting and Food Rituals — Examples:

➤ Fast on nine consecutive Saturdays, with the permission of your medical professional.

➤ On nine consecutive Saturdays, or nine consecutive days, starting on Saturday refrain from eating junk foods, leftovers, dark colored foods, coffee, chocolate, rye bread, or other foods related to ES9.

➤ Give the above foods to ES9/Ketu people as charity.

➤ Alternately, go out of your way to eat ES9/Ketu foods on Saturdays, particularly those that are not a regular part of your diet.

Other Rituals — Examples:

On Saturdays, do one or more of the following activities:

➤ Use sesame seeds or red lentils to draw the shape of a flag on a pole on the ground in front of your door, on your altar, back patio or near your trashcans. You can also sing ES9 *mantras* while you do this, and you can surround your image with items related to ES9/Ketu.

➤ Place a translucent, yellow-orange glass filled with water in the sunlight on Saturday mornings. Drink the water in the evening to ingest ES9/Ketu influences via the light through the colored glass.

CAUTION: Do not do this activity if you are afflicted by ES9 Problems. It is only for enhancing Qualities of ES9. Stop if you begin to see problems.

Creative Homage — Examples:

On Saturdays, do one or more of the following activities:

> ➤ Draw, paint, sculpt, or create needlework to make an image of a famous poor monk or nun, like St. Francis of Assisi, Mother Theresa, Poor Clare, Mahatma Gandhi, or of renowned fishermen, including Christ or his disciples.

> ➤ Create the above picture using *"Mantra* Painting," – writing tiny, curving ES9/Ketu *mantras* in place of penciled lines and solid blocks of color.

> ➤ Use honey colors, light iced-tea colors and similar shades of yellow brown to create the above image.

> ➤ Sing or silently say ES9/Ketu *mantras* while you work.

> ➤ Compose and sing a song honoring any of the correspondences of ES9.

Healing Stories — Examples:

On Saturdays, do one or more of the following activities:

> ➤ Read stories or biographies of a famous poor monk or nun, like St. Francis of Assisi, Mother Theresa, Poor Clare, Mahatma Gandhi, or of renowned fishermen, including John the Baptist, and Jesus or his disciples.

> ➤ Or write your own stories about the above figures.

> ➤ Create and produce puppet plays about an owl, a fisherman, John the Baptist, a wandering saint, or other archetypes of ES9.

Mantras and Prayers:

Select one of the *mantras* from the list below. While you may recite these *mantras* on any day, be <u>sure</u> to do it on Saturdays. When Sanskrit is available, use Sanskrit. Translations do not carry the same vibrational power.

Seed *Mantra*

- OM sraam sreem sraum sah ketuve namah.

Simple *Mantra*

OM Hum Kum Ketuve Namaha.

Ketu Gayatri *Mantra*

OM Aswadhwa jaaya Vidmahe
Shoola hastaaya Dheemahi
Dhano Ketu, Prachodayat.

(translation)

Let me meditate on Ketu,
He who has a trident in his hand.
Let Ketu enlighten me.

Other *Mantra*

OM Palasha pushpa sankasham
Taraka-grahu masta-kam
Rowdram row-drat makam goram
Tam keytoom prana-mammya-ham.

(translation)

I offer my honors to the violent and fearsome Ketu,
Who is endowed with the potency of Lord Shiva.
Resembling in his complexion
The flower of a palasa plant,
He serves as the head of the stars and planets.

Prayer

Lord, let me be the instrument of thy will.

Pujas and *Yagyas:*

Contact www.puja.net or www.amma.org to arrange *pujas* or *yagyas*.

11. BALANCING TRANSCENDENT ENERGY SYSTEMS

The Vedas deal only with the Energy Systems of planets that are visible to the naked eye. This makes sense for a discipline called *"Jyotish,"* meaning "the science of light." Yet followers of western astrology are very aware of the Energy Systems of the "outer planets:" Uranus, Neptune, and Pluto. Transcendent Energy Systems require our consciousness -- specifically, our conscious awareness of autonomy, authenticity, spirituality, and willing surrender to a higher power.

An important distinction exists between these categories of Energy Systems. While the visible planets address the physical world in which we live and the Moon's Nodes reflect desires and acceptance, the outer planets offer us spiritual growth. Their energies enhance our ability to negotiate the physical world by adding advanced awareness and the use of higher levels of consciousness. It's been said that many techniques used by psychology to change or enhance our lives would have been indistinguishable from Magic in ancient times. Psychological techniques often reflect conscious awareness applied to life situations. When we refuse to apply the gift of higher awareness, the outer planets' Energy Systems can wreak havoc with our lives.

In astrological thinking, the discovery of a new planet offers humanity the opportunity to become consciously aware of a new kind of energy for the first time. We see examples of this in history.

Uranus, the planet of freedom, rebellion, individual authenticity and autonomy was discovered in 1781, coinciding with the cry for individual rights of the American and French revolutions. The rallying cry was freedom and dignity for everyone—not just the rich. Personal autonomy seems to be a prerequisite for spiritual awakening.

Neptune is the epitome of non-physical energies. It was discovered in 1846, and its profound interior essence was demonstrated by the beginnings of psychology in the years immediately following Neptune's discovery. This was also a time of great spiritual movements, with séances, physical mediums and psychic phenomenon of all kinds becoming quite the rage. This also marked the beginning of mass movements toward spirituality, as opposed to simply following religious dogma.

Pluto, the planet of ultimate power that takes us to our knees and then releases us to a greater level of existence, was discovered in 1930, on the eve of nuclear weaponry, the Holocaust, and the cruelest world war imaginable. Humanity had a close look into the underworld during these dark years. Pluto forces us to face our most profound fears.

Over the past several years, astronomers have been re-classifying planets, moving Pluto into the category of "dwarf planet" and discovering several other large objects in the Kuiper Belt. We don't yet have enough experience with the newly identified Energy Systems to know how they will affect us. It is interesting to note that the new Kuiper Belt objects are all being named after Creation Gods from multiple cultures. Since there seems to be an odd and inexplicable link between the mythologies behind planets' names and their influence on our lives on earth, there may be new hope for creating a better world over the coming decades. Nevertheless, there are as yet no balancing activities for these energies.

The format and style of the activities sections for ES10/Uranus, ES11/Neptune and ES12/Pluto is different from the format used for the traditional Energy Systems. Obviously, there were no traditional Vedic *mantras* designed for these planets. You will find sections on Conceptual Balancing and Ideas to Ponder, which offer introspective ways of relating to these systems.

The activities for the Transcendental Planets are based on principles derived from traditional balancing activities. While these activities are new, they are still extremely valid and effective. I use them often, and so do many of my clients.

BALANCING ENERGY SYSTEM 10/URANUS

ES10/URANUS Table of Correspondences

SHAPE: Lightning bolt.

WEEKDAY: No particular day and when you least expect it.

DIVINITIES: Prometheus, Ouranos/Uranus.

PEOPLE: Contraries (Native American individualists),
            rebels, unconventional persons, oddballs and
            eccentrics, mentally unstable persons, visionaries,
            astrologers, revolutionaries, anarchists, those
            who put principles above persons, electricians,
            computer specialists, new age thinkers, futurists,
            electronic media specialists, "Save the _____"
            (fill in the blank) groups, alternative lifestyle
            persons, "energy" healers.

PARTS OF BODY: Central nervous system, ankles,
            parathyroid gland, the aura.

ANIMALS: Mosquitoes (flight pattern), electric eels, fireflies,
            pileated woodpeckers, any erratic, electrical, or
            light-producing animals.

PLANTS: Plants that break "plant rules": *e.g.* air plants like
            stag-horn ferns, "sensitive plants" that react to
            touch, meat-eating plants like Venus fly traps.

PLACES: Technology centers, alternative lifestyle centers,
            TV stations, internet hubs, earthquake fault lines.

GEMS AND MINERALS: Bright blue turquoise, Paraiba
            tourmaline, neon apatite, prehnite, any stone that
            glows in the dark, moldavite (from meteors),
            copper and zinc.

COLORS: Electric blue, bright blue turquoise.

BALANCING ACTIVITIES

Charity and Service — Examples:

➢ Give rechargeable batteries to a computer or gadget geek.

➢ Give a glowing statue or sculpture (neon or naturally fluorescent) to a new-age retreat center.

➢ Give oddball trinkets to an eccentric.

➢ Send a shocking computer file to a media outlet.

➢ Give an astrology chart, reading, or report to an open-minded person.

➢ Use the ES10/Uranus Table of Correspondences to mix and match your own charities and services.

Rituals and Activities — Examples:

➢ Deliberately dress in an odd or unexpected way (for you) and go to a public event.

➢ Turn lights, fans, or other electrical appliances on while you sleep (particularly useful for insomnia).

➢ Leave a radio, repeating CD or mp3 player, television, book-on-tape, or other sound device playing while you sleep (particularly useful for insomnia).

➢ Wear socks of two dramatically different colors.

➢ Wear two dramatic, and dramatically mismatched, earrings and see if anyone notices.

➢ Learn how to operate a new electronic device.

➢ Add streaks of electric blue to your hair.

➢ Get a "new age energy healing."

➢ Deliberately shock someone with an oddball idea.

➢ Draw a lightning bolt outside your front door, near your computer table, television or electronic entertainment center, using neon chalk if you can. You may also place objects related to ES10/Uranus energies around the image.

Creative Homage — Examples:

➢ Draw, paint, dance, or create music utilizing the colors, objects, energies, and principles of Uranus/Prometheus.

➢ Create a dance that imitates the jerky flight pattern of a mosquito.

➢ Learn how to breakdance and practice it, in front of someone if you can.

Healing Stories — Examples:

➢ Read (or write) stories relating to Uranus/Prometheus or historic persons who represent this archetype (revolutionaries, people who changed the course of the world with their new ideas — like Steve Jobs, *etc.*).

➢ The fabulous epic and autobiographical novel, **Shantaram**, by Gregory David Roberts, is a paean to finding freedom within. This is obvious from the very first paragraph. Read it!

➢ Write an autobiography about a time in your life when you came to a radical new understanding of yourself that freed you from a previous set of assumptions.

Conceptual Balancing:

Energy System 10/Uranus governs our fear of losing freedom, autonomy, and individuality. When this ES is triggered, it causes knee-jerk over-reactions. The phrases "I don't need this. I'm outta here!" and "Take this job and SHOVE it!" are pure ES10 statements. As a planet, Uranus is truly an oddball. It rolls sideways and spins backwards compared to the other planets. ES10/Uranus is truly a "contrary" in Native American parlance.

Usually we gain understandings of planetary ESs by examining the mythology of the planet's name, though in the quirky case of Uranus, Dr. Richard Tarnas demonstrates Uranus is different here as well. He makes an exquisite case that the meaningful archetype for this ES is the story of Prometheus. Prometheus was the Titan who believed that the gods shouldn't have all the goodies, leaving humans in the dark. Prometheus sneaked into the gods' abode and stole the secret of fire AND the secret of creating new life, earning their everlasting enmity. Prometheus was the prototypical revolutionary on behalf of humanity.

The most typical reaction to difficult Uranus energies is to feel that your autonomy has been abrogated and that you MUST get free, no matter what. It's a "cut off your nose to spite your face" decision-making process that causes people to destroy something they love because one little problem makes them feel trapped. Because this energy is so restless and highly charged, another typical reaction is that your thoughts begin to feel like a swarm of mosquitoes clogging your brain, dividing your attention, harassing you and making it difficult to concentrate or to sleep. This is when you lie awake because you can't remember WHAT was the name of the boy who sat next to Jennifer in the third grade. What an annoying mosquito-thought!

The way to balance this ES is to learn that the only person who can truly take your freedom is yourself. The only person who can harness the mosquitoes in your brain is you — and it's helpful first to get in touch with your real self.

Freedom is defined by authenticity. If you are itching to get out of a troublesome situation, if you are impatient and want your life to change radically, the real challenge is the assumption that something <u>outside</u> of you is preventing you from being fully you. It's easy to think that being authentic means getting away from something you reject. It's far more important to move positively toward an expression of who you are. Usually it's easier to know what you DON'T want than to know what you DO want.

Ideas to Ponder:

➤ What parts of yourself are you hiding from others?

- Why are you hiding them?

- What would happen if you expressed them?

- Is there a time and place for you to express these hidden parts of yourself? If so, do so.

➤ What do you dare not say aloud?

- What would happen if you did?

- Why are you staying silent?

- Is there a time and place for you to begin to say these things? If so, do so.

➤ Do you feel that you are not doing what you want to with your life, and that you just want to quit the old stuff?

- Before you quit, identify what you DO want to do with your life.

- Experiment with the new before quitting the old (unless we're talking about spouses).

- Be aware that resisting something is the negative side of creating something new for yourself.

- Take classes in subjects that have always interested you but that you have never made the time for.

➢ If swarms of mosquito-thoughts are keeping you awake at night, sit up and make note of them.

- Do these thoughts have anything in common?

- Do they point to a time, place, or experience in which you were authentically YOU?

- Are these thoughts trying to distract you from actions that will create new excitement in your life? What might those actions be?

Ultimately, freedom comes from within. The hero in **_Shantaram_** finds, while being chained and beaten, he still has the freedom to hate or to forgive, and he knows the choice he makes will change his life. We all have the inner freedom to think and BE our own authentic self. Even if life circumstances don't allow you to express all of yourself externally, ES10/Uranus is a wake-up call to know your inner self more thoroughly.

BALANCING ENERGY SYSTEM 11/NEPTUNE

ES11/NEPTUNE Table of Correspondences

SHAPE: Infinity sign.

WEEKDAY: All days.

DIVINITIES: Maya, Neptune, Dionysius, Pan, Bacchus.

PEOPLE: Mystics, idealists, actors and actresses, anyone
             associated with movies or theaters, pharmacists,
             barkeepers, spiritual healers, alcoholics, drug
             addicts, drug dealers or drug salespersons (legal
             or illegal), con-artists, oil company workers,
             mega-stars, anesthesiologists, psychics,
             glamorous people, fishing people, musicians,
             illusionists, confused or deluded people, public
             relations experts, advertisers, liars, hypnotists.

PARTS OF BODY: Pineal gland, soles of the feet.

ANIMALS: Sea creatures, dolphins, slugs, jellyfish, and other
             skin-less, spine-less, shell-less creatures.

PLANTS: Morning glories, weeping willow trees, lavender,
             hypnogogic plants, lotuses, water lilies, seaweed,
             algae, water-growing plants.

PLACES: Spiritual retreat centers, theaters, film sets,
             seashores, oceans, ocean-liners, large lakes, boats,
             marshes, bogs, swamps, watery places, foggy
             places, places of contagion, oil barges and
             refineries.

GEMS AND MINERALS: Opal, silver.

COLORS: Green-blue, aqua, misty and foggy colors.

216

BALANCING ACTIVITIES

Charity and Service — Examples:

➤ Give (or get) a "spiritual healing."

➤ Bring a seashell to the seashore and offer it to the sea.

➤ Give a bottle of wine to a theater-buff. Or buy a drink for a PR (public relations) person.

➤ Confuse a confuser.

➤ Take a mystic to a movie, or take a movie to a mystic.

➤ Give a gauzy, filmy green-blue piece of cloth to a psychic — or to a confused person.

➤ Share a meal of seafood with a mystic, alcoholic, or dreamer.

➤ Sense the energy around you and act on any messages you may receive.

Rituals and Activities — Examples:

➤ Meditate. This is the best way to reach the highest expression of ES11/Neptune. Meditation provides a boundary-less contact with All-That-Is. DO NOT use meditation to escape from your real life.

➤ Listen to soothing music. Sing!

➤ For at least four hours (best is one full day), OBEY the inner voice that whispers things for you to do. For example, while your arms are up to the elbow in engine grease you may think "Go to the grocery store." This means, "Do it NOW," not fifteen minutes from now. Do whatever comes to your mind the moment you think of it. You will be amazed at how much you can accomplish in this non-linear way! (Obviously, any actions that could harm others should be avoided. This level of awareness also requires the highest integrity.)

➢ Draw an infinity symbol outside your door using water, oil, or alcohol. Surround it with items related to ES11.

➢ Write down (or better, audio-record) your night-time dreams.

➢ Write down (or better, audio-record) your dreams for your life.

➢ Remember what it feels like to fall in love.

➢ Spend an hour fantasizing—about anything that pleases you.

➢ Use essential oils.

Creative Homage — Examples:

➢ Build a puppet theater. Use your most magically inspired imagination to decorate it. Create puppets and make up and perform plays.

➢ Draw, paint, dance, or create music utilizing the colors, energies, objects, shapes, and principles of ES11/Neptune.

Healing Stories — Examples:

➢ Read stories and mythologies that relate to ES11/ Neptune, or read about famous historic persons who represent this archetype, like Theresa of Avila, Mother Meera, Elizabeth Taylor, Joshua Bell, Placido Domingo, Harry Houdini, Marilyn Monroe and other famous mystics, film stars, musicians.

➢ Write your own story about the above ES11 people.

➢ Read or write fairy tales.

> ➤ Make up the most romantic story you can possibly imagine and write it down. Or make it into a movie.

Conceptual Balancing:

ES11/Neptune represents everything intangible and separated from material reality. It also represents our need to escape reality. ES11 is active if you simply can't face the real work of the day, preferring to spend time and energy on escapism. It is also active in the lives of musicians and creators of the alternate realities of television, film, and theater. In daily life, compulsive reading, TV- or movie-watching, drinking alcohol and taking drugs are part of this archetype. So is addiction to meditation. All of these take one away from the "cold hard world."

ES11 is about dreams and ideals, which by Platonic definition can never be fully material. Plato says what we think is real is only a shadow observed by cavemen who, seeing shadows dance on the wall of the cave, think they are reality. The cavemen have no full idea of the reality of objects casting the shadows. ES11 makes you believe you can see the *uber*-reality behind the world of illusion. The danger is to believe your vision *exists* or *could be solid* in physical reality.

By definition, ideals are NOT "bricks-and-mortar" real. They are our imagination of perfection. *Perfect* is something else we don't find in physical reality, except in singular moments that are short in duration. The painting you imagine is always better than the painting you paint. You may have a moment of "perfect" understanding, or may make the "perfect" basketball play, but these are elusive and passing experiences. When you believe your ideal can take lasting form in the physical world, you are setting the stage for profound disappointment and disillusionment. When you base your life on this belief, you guarantee a fall.

The heady, "walking on air" experience of falling in love is a perfect example of an ES11 experience. ES11/Neptune is the dream we never want to give up, whether it's perfect love or the business idea that will cost you nothing, make you millions and save the planet. We resist anything that might shatter a potent dream of this nature. Have you ever tried to tell a person, head over heels in love, that his or her beloved is the worst possible partnership choice? Even if the whole rest of the world can see it, that person will not.

But ES11 is not all bad. It is responsible for our most ecstatic experiences of universal "oneness" — the dissolution of all boundaries between the Self and God, or All-That-Is. This ES offers us profound psychic abilities, mystical visions, and ecstatic revelations of spirit. Such information is difficult to integrate into normal life but enriches the spirit.

Because ES11 takes us away from bricks and mortar reality, it is common for persons experiencing it to feel they're living in a fog. They can't see where they're going in life. If you are driving your car in a profound fog, what should you do? If you can't see ahead for other traffic or signage, your only recourse is to slow down, watch the little white line at the side of the road next to you, and get off the road as soon as you can. Then wait until the fog passes – or until you get a "message." Then it's safe to move forward again.

Ideas to Ponder:

➤ Think of life as the children's game, sometimes called a "Treasure Hunt." In this game, a child is told there is a present waiting at the end of the game if she follows instructions. Then she is given a note that says something like "look under the front door-mat." Under the mat will be another note that says, "Go to Mrs. Smith's apple tree." The apple tree will have a note dangling from a string that says something like "look under the swings in your back yard."

At no time does the child know where he will end up or what will be waiting there. All the child knows is that following the immediate instructions will bring him to something good. Playing this game teaches us to trust the messages of the moment.

- Design a treasure hunt game for special people in your life.

- Watch these people adapt their thinking as they first begin to trust that, without knowing where they're going, something good awaits them.

➢ Imagine you have, in addition to your five physical senses, a powerful new sense organ that takes the form of invisible antennae. These antennae are fuzzy and sensitive, like bug antennae, and can pick up subtle energy signals around you.

- Any "messages" you receive in this state will be absolutely true — ONLY for the moment of your realization.

- When you receive the message of the moment (*e.g.* "call my mother- in- law"), the message means, "DO IT NOW", not in ten minutes or two days. (Obviously, any action that could harm others should always be avoided. This level of awareness requires the highest levels of integrity.)

- When you receive the message "Doing THIS activity gives my life meaning," it means FOR THIS MOMENT. It doesn't mean, "therefore I should plan my life around it." (The biggest danger signal for ES11 is the use of the word "therefore." ES11 energies are not designed for planning ahead.)

- By using your "bug antennae", you can count on the insights of the moment FOR that moment. If you act upon the insights immediately, with discipline and integrity they will lead you to the right future for you.

➢ If you feel stuck in escapism or a foggy mental state, first engage your bug antennae to see if there is anything you need to do right now.

- If so, do it.

- If not, change your current activity, selecting any of the Balancing Activities for ES11.

- Or, do something practical, pragmatic, and grounded in the physical world: balance your checkbook or clean the cupboards.

- Or take a nap and make note of your dreams.

BALANCING ENERGY SYSTEM 12/PLUTO

ES11/PLUTO Table of Correspondences

SHAPE:	Torus (a dynamic, doughnut-like shape).
WEEKDAY:	No specific day, stronger on Tuesday and Saturday.
DIVINITIES:	Pluto, Hades, the phoenix bird, Yama (Hindu god of death), Nataraja (Dancing Shiva), Quaoar (Native American). (Nataraja and Quaoar are both gods who destroy the world then dance it back to life.) Mother Theresa (saint who worked with the dying).
PEOPLE:	Extremely powerful people, underworld figures, gangsters, white collar criminals, corporate bandits, people who transform the world, people who have near death experiences, hospice workers, oil company and pharmaceutical executives, true (not stage) magicians, detectives, spies, arms dealers, miners, executioners, depth psychologists, researchers, doctors who deal with life and death, surgeons, gemstone miners, occultists, sexually obsessed persons, manipulators, nuclear researchers.
PARTS OF BODY:	Pancreas, the metabolism, elimination system, sexual organs.
ANIMALS:	Phoenix, snakes, scorpions, eagles, doves, raptors, moles and underground animals.
PLANTS:	The first plants of spring: (crocuses, hyacinths, daffodils, snowdrops), nightshades and poisonous plants, hypnogogic, entheogenic and psychotropic plants.

PLACES: World Trade Centers, stock markets, big banks, halls of power, transformational healing centers, hospices, gemstone trade centers, big oil and gas companies, power companies, nuclear power plants, sewage processing centers, cemeteries.

GEMS AND MINERALS: Jet, black diamond, black onyx, marcasite, platinum, moldavite, volcanic gemstones.

COLORS: Black, dark silvery gray, dark blood red.

BALANCING ACTIVITIES

Charity and Service — Examples:

➤ Give something you treasure to a person who is dying.

➤ Give something you value to someone you believe doesn't deserve it.

➤ Sort through your possessions, ruthlessly weeding out anything you haven't used recently, and donate the rest to a hospice group or to a *wealthy* charity.

➤ Attend a prestigious charity function.

Rituals and Activities — Examples:

➤ Go through your files, paperwork, garage, attic, closets and throw away everything that has no value to anyone. Give away everything that has no immediate use to you.

➤ Make your will. Seriously. Plan your funeral.

➤ Create and tend a compost heap on Saturdays.

➤ Meditate on the concept of divine will, and how to apply this concept in your own life: "Not my will, but Thine, be done."

➤ Meditate over the body of a dead person or animal.

➤ Study nuclear physics. Research the effects of atomic bombs.

➤ Research the physical energy properties of the *torus*.

➤ Do one thing each week that brings you great joy. This doesn't mean treating yourself because you need a reward for suffering. This means <u>Deliberately Experience Ecstatic Joy!!</u>

➤ Make a list of things that make you "who you are." This can include your clothing style, beliefs, a favorite piece of jewelry, the way you relate to your career, or your children.

  ▪ Pretend you no longer have these things.

  ▪ Each week, change something related to one of those items.

➤ Follow your bliss!

➤ Take a risk and do something you always dreamed of doing.

➤ Burn something you value, reminding yourself of the importance of surrender to a higher power and the illusion of permanence.

Creative Homage — Examples:

➢ Draw, paint, dance, or create music honoring the stories of Pluto and Persephone, Sita and Rama, or Nataraja (The Dancing Shiva), or the story of the Native American god Quaoar, utilizing the darkest of red colors, dark grey, black, and using the objects and other principles of ES12/Pluto.

➢ Paint images of the phoenix. Use ES12 colors and the Mrityunjaya *Mantra*.

➢ Take time out, doing nothing else, to listen <u>intently</u> to Mozart's **Requiem**, Gabriel Faure's **Requiem**, or other great requiem masses. Listen for all the background instruments and voices.

➢ Study the Hispanic customs of *El Dia De Los Muertos*, "The Day of the Dead." (This is celebrated on November 1st, though preparations are made long in advance.)

   ▪ Make skeleton-shaped foods and puppets.

   ▪ Create an altar to your dead ancestors and loved ones, and decorate it with images of death.

➢ Become obsessed with finding JOY, or with doing something that gives you JOY.

Healing Stories — Examples:

➤ Read the mythologies of Pluto and Persephone, Hades, Innana, Sita and Rama. Write your own versions of these stories.

➤ Read stories about the mythological phoenix, or write new ones.

➤ Read about Christ's resurrection, or read stories about those who have hit bottom and risen into positions of glory.

➤ Read biographies, or write your own essays about robber barons, the extremely wealthy, (such as Bill Gates or Warren Buffet), world transformers such as Mahatma Gandhi, Steven Jobs, Nelson Mandela.

➤ Read biographies of journalists who specialize in dangerous situations, risking death to find their stories.

➤ Read Dante's *__Divine Comedy__* (The Inferno, Purgatorio, Paradiso), and write your own commentary about the journey from Inferno to Paradise.

Conceptual Balancing:

Some people are born with the intensity of ES12/Pluto. For these people, life is empty without great journeys of trial and transformation. Others encounter this energy only periodically during a lifetime and are terrified by it. ES12 is always about confronting a power greater than Self and letting go of something we value excessively. Letting go of an identity is like a mini-death, threatening something in life that is of utmost importance to us. Faced with threats to our identity, we may feel like life itself is ending. We can't see beyond the abyss. Nevertheless, ES12 energy always has a higher purpose: the threats come to us when we have gotten so comfortable in some area (an area where we are stuck) that we are unable to see new opportunities and unable to grow. If it's time to step out of the comfort zone, ES12 will make sure you get out.

When we are finally forced to let go of safety, we discover a new world we could never have imagined before our dark journey. Invariably, people will say, "I never want to go through that again, but now that it's over I'm glad it happened -- because otherwise I never would have found _____, which is the best thing that ever happened to me."

When ES12 energy first approaches us, it usually brings a nagging sense of dissatisfaction with current circumstances. If that dissatisfaction doesn't lead you to make dramatic and deliberate changes in that area of life, the existing circumstances will inexorably deteriorate. You may feel victimized and outraged by blatantly unfair treatment and wish to rectify the injustice or fight back. You are probably justified in believing the situation is outrageously unfair. However, in these circumstances, there is no gain in being "right." You have no power in this situation—the other guy has it all. If you fight, you will lose more than you will gain.

Some people live their whole lives this way. If you are constantly subject to abuses from people who have power over you, it's critical to learn the remedies for ES12/Pluto. Harmonizing with this energy will lead to your own personal resurrection.

Ultimately, ES12/Pluto teaches us that the self we are accustomed to is a false identity. Who we think we are is only the tiniest portion of who we can be. ES12 forces us to leave this small identity behind. Just as the seed drops its casing to grow into a new plant, we must abandon our outgrown selves to enter a greater reality. When this change is embraced, the forces of the universe open to make dreams come true.

Ideas to Ponder:

➤ Who are you? How would you describe yourself? Imagine how you would identify yourself if all you know were taken away.

➤ What is the most important thing in your life? WHO would you be without it? Before you are asked to sacrifice this thing, practice living as if it were no longer there. For example, if the most important thing is "your children", make time to do adult things that don't involve your children. If the most important thing is "your career", make time to do things for pleasure only. If the most important thing is "your religion", make time for some purely secular entertainment. Do these activities NOW. Not later.

➤ Ask yourself if you really have any power in this situation. For example, you may have the law on your side, but if your opponent has the political power or money to keep you in court for the next hundred years, do you really have any power? Acknowledge to yourself – and especially acknowledge to your enemies -- when you are powerless.

➢ Recognize that the only power you have is POWER OVER YOURSELF. You can control your behaviors, words, and over-reactions. You can walk away from a bad situation. You don't have to fight. Alternately, you can decide to stay and suffer. Whatever you decide, fighting the situation won't help.

➢ What are you being asked to sacrifice? (Hint: Ultimately, it's your ego.)

➢ Acknowledge to those who oppose you that you are powerless to change their minds.

➢ Acknowledge to your boss that he or she IS the boss, <u>especially</u> if you think she's wrong.

➢ Write an autobiographical story about your own journey into the darkness and the light you discovered at its center.

Mantras and Prayers:

Select one of the *mantras* from the list below. When Sanskrit is available, use Sanskrit. Translations do not carry the same vibrational power. While you may repeat the *mantras* on any day, be sure to do it on Saturdays.

Simple *Mantras*

Not my will, but Thine be done.
Luke, 22:42

Lord, help me be an instrument of Thy will.

Mrityunjaya *Mantra*

OM, Tryumbakam yayamahe,
Shugandhim pushti Vardhanam.
Urdvaru Kamiva Bandhanan.
Mrityor, Mukshiya mam ritad.

(translation)

We meditate on Shiva
The three-eyed one of sweet fragrance,
Who expands spiritual growth.
Like the fully-ripened fruit drops from its stem
May I be free from the bondage of death
And attachment in life,
But not from immortality.

Tibetan *Mantra*

Gahtay, gahtay, para gahtay
Para sum gahtay
Bodhi swaha.

(translation)

Gone, gone, gone beyond,
Gone beyond the beyond
To the shores of enlightenment.

The Serenity Prayer

God grant me the serenity
to accept the things I cannot change;
courage to change the things I can;
and wisdom to know the difference.

Reinhold Niebuhr

PART IV:

Wrapping It Up

Illustration 5

Six Days of Creation and Redemption

SILK TAPESTRY BY ANNE BEVERSDORF
Based on a vision of HILDEGARD VON BINGEN.

In Hildegard's visions, the six days of creation are capped by the redeeming solar disc, suggesting the ultimate power of the seven. Here we are reminded of the seven days for performing energy balancing activities to create new worlds of our own.

Color image may be viewed at:
http://www.sacred-threads.com/tapestries-2/hildegard-von-bingen-inspired/six-days-of-creation/

"Six Days of Creation and Redemption"

12. WHO DID WHAT

This book opened with stories about people who applied balancing activities to ward off trouble, reduce problems, and generally make their lives happier. In case you are wondering what they did, here is the "rest of the story."

> In the first case, I was suffering from depression. I studied my chart from the perspective of Jyotish, and realized that ES7/Saturn was too heavy and needed lightening up. ES4/Mercury was getting squished and needed support. ES5/Jupiter was in a weak position, damaging my optimism, and ES2/Moon was isolated. So I had *pujas* done for Saturn, Mercury, Jupiter and Moon by Ammaji. My depression lifted in a most amazing way.

> Jim's happiest love life was during the time when he, unknowingly, was balancing ES6/Venus energies by bringing flowers to the secretaries he worked with. In his own chart, secretaries are symbols also related to

237

"partnership" and the ES6 activities were archetypal activities to create love.

➢ Caroline regained her relationship with her father and helped her daughter get back on track by balancing ES5/Jupiter, which is related both to one's father and to one's children. She gave yellow flowers to a wise man on Thursdays.

➢ When my brother and mother were in danger because of his wife's mental illness, we did *pujas* and *yagyas* recommended by Ben Collins at *www.puja.net.* I recited *mantras* for hours daily, including the *Mrityunjaya* and ES3/Mars *mantras* to support my brother.

➢ Lucy broke her poverty streak by selling a multi-million dollar property just a week after doing *yagyas* recommended by Ben Collins.

➢ Matt had been downsized three times in three years. He had entered a Mars Dasa just before he lost the first job. ES3/Mars was extraordinarily weak in his Vedic chart, so he started throwing cinnamon "red hots" into running streams on Tuesdays. Two weeks later he got a good offer and his headaches, a secondary issue, also related to ES3/Mars, finally ended.

➢ Jeanne, as grandparent and daytime caregiver for her granddaughter, was in a position to "help" directly. The child's chart showed a dangerous combination of ES7/Saturn with ES4/Mercury, both related to her grandchild's vitality. In cooperation with the parents, she played tapes of ES4/ Mercury and ES7/Saturn *mantras* day and night in the baby's room. She also fed sunflower seeds to ravens on Saturdays and cleaned trash from an empty lot near her home.

➤ Rachel had a very strange pattern in her Vedic chart. She was in the *dasa* time-period of Mars/Saturn. At the same time, in the sky, those two planets were coming together in the part of her birth chart representing her daughter. This pattern repeated in the chart representing Rachel's children in general. Furthermore, her Mars and Saturn were being challenged by other planetary movements, all during the ten-day period of the Iditarod.

Rachel addressed ES3/Mars by giving red flowers to firefighters on Tuesdays, addressed ES7/Saturn by taking dark colored foods to elderly shut-ins on Saturdays and feeding sunflower seeds to crows. Her daughter emerged from the predicted accident unscathed.

➤ Beverly started doing *mantras* for ES3/Mars (fire). In her Vedic chart, Jupiter and Venus were setting up the problem, so she addressed ES6/Venus by giving scented flowers to young girls on Fridays and addressed ES5/Jupiter by giving yellow flowers to her father on Thursdays. The expected fire barely scorched the kitchen paint.

➤ Jason was about to enter a Saturn/Rahu *dasa* period, associated in his Vedic chart with bankruptcy, chronic illness, loss, and death. As a child, he experienced a Rahu/Saturn *dasa*, which was virtually the same energy pattern. In childhood, he instinctually began visiting a reclusive old woman on Saturdays. This happens to be an exact remedy for the ES7/Saturn and ES8/Rahu energy systems. I recommended he visit recluses on Saturdays this time, or again trust his obviously excellent instincts.

➤ Since Sally's problems seemed to involve gynecological issues, she addressed them with ES2/Moon activities. For nine consecutive Mondays she walked to a nearby church and lit a candle to the Virgin Mary. By the end of the nine weeks, new and helpful medical information became available.

13. YOUR NEXT STEP

Now is the time for you to put the book down and fix your shopping cart. If you've ever felt you've been driving down the aisles of your life with a broken wheel, you now have the tools to repair it.

REMEMBER THE BASICS:

> ➤ Start with one activity. Add more later.

> ➤ Do the activity on the appropriate weekday.

> ➤ For emergencies, do it nine days in a row.

> ➤ In general, do it nine weeks in a row.

> ➤ For long-term problems, do the activity for as many weeks as your age, plus one more week.

> ➤ From the Table of Correspondences for the specific Energy System, mix and match to give the "right" things to the "right" people, places, deities, or animals.

> ➢ You can do *mantras* at any time. Do them so often they get stuck in your head like a pop song or advertising jingle.

The activities in this book only scratch the surface of what is possible. If this book were complete, it would be as vast as the universe. Virtually everything in the universe will correspond to one or more of the twelve Energy Systems. You can spend hours on the web finding more *mantras* for each of the Energy Systems, and the kinds of activities you can devise for each ES are limited only by your imagination.

The Appendices include good "general purpose" *mantras*, prayers, and sources for *pujas* and *yagyas*. If you memorize *mantras*, you'll always have spiritual help in an emergency. The Appendices also include a cross-reference for matching problems and remedies, and a quick-reference guide to activities for each system. The Bibliography that follows offers more background information and more inspiration and practices for balancing your life.

As you direct your attention to the great, interlocking wheels of energy systems and remedies, you will discover a growing awareness of the interconnectedness of everything in the universe around you. The correspondences between our life experiences and the great energy wheels will write itself in the world you see, making it possible to feel the winds of change when they are only breezes, and to harmonize your life with ease and grace.

I wish you the very best in making your life-dance as beautiful and pleasing as possible.

Appendices

APPENDIX A:

GENERAL PURPOSE
MANTRAS AND PRAYERS

Some *mantras* and prayers are so widely used and highly respected that they can be applied to many life situations. The suggested uses only touch the surface for times to use each prayer or *mantra*. Listen to your heart, and use those that call to you at any given time. Here is a group of them in a single location for your convenience.

You can find free mp3 audio files for most of these mantras under **Stariel Press** at the website, **www.stariel.com**

<u>Ganesha *Mantra*</u>
(To remove obstacles, find wisdom, happiness, abundance)

OM Gum Ganapataye Namaha.

Shiva *Mantra*
(To relieve distress.)

OM Namo Shivaya.

Ganesha *Mantra*
(To remove obstacles, find wisdom, happiness, abundance)

OM Gum Ganapataye Namaha.

Navagraha *Mantra*
(Mantra honoring all nine traditional energy systems — good for all-purpose balancing.)

Brahma Murari stri purantu karve
Bhanu Sashi Bhoomi-Sutra Budhascha
Guruscha Sukra Sani Rahu Ketuva
Kurvante Sarve Mam-Sutra Bhataam.

(Praise for the Sun, Moon, the five planets and Rahu and Ketu.)

Mrityunjaya *Mantra*
(To relieve acute distress of all kinds.)

OM, Tryumbakam yayamahe
Shugandhim pushti Vardhanam
Urdvaru Kamiva Bandhanan
Mrityor, Mukshiya Mam ritad.

(translation)

We meditate on Shiva,
The three-eyed one of sweet fragrance,
Who expands spiritual growth.
Like the fully-ripened fruit drops from its stem
May I be free from the bondage of death
and attachment in life,
But not from immortality.

Ganapati *Mantra*
(For abundance, joy, and spiritual growth.)

OM Gananan-tva,
Ganapatiqum Havamahe,
Kavin kavin-am
Upama sravastamam
Jyesthara-jam Brahmanam
Brahmana spata Anas srinvan,
Nutibhis si Dasadanam
Sri MahaGanapataye, Namaha.

(Come and sit near us and hear our prayers to remove
obstacles to love, wisdom, and abundance.)

Gatayri *Mantra*
(To support optimism, leadership ability, growth.)

OM Bhur Bhuvah Swaha
Tat Savitur Varenyam
Vargo, Devasya Dheemahi
Dhiyo yo nah, Prachodayat.

(translation)

Earth, Atmosphere, Heavens
We meditate on the sacred light
Of the effulgent source.
Let that inspire our thoughts.

Doxology
(For confidence, faith, and appreciation of life.)

Praise God from Whom All Blessings Flow
Praise Him All Creatures here below
Praise Him above ye Heavenly Hosts
Praise Father, Son and Holy Ghost.
Amen.

The Lord's Prayer

(For inner peace, appreciation, trust.)

Our Father which art in Heaven
Hallowed by Thy Name
Thy Kingdom Come, Thy Will Be Done
On Earth as it is in Heaven
Give us this day our daily bread
And forgive us our debts as we forgive our debtors.
Lead us not into temptation
But deliver us from evil,
For Thine is the Kingdom, the Power,
And the Glory Forever.
Amen.

Old Testament Prayer

(For courage, endurance, faith.)

They that wait upon the LORD
Shall renew their strength;
They shall mount up with wings as eagles;
They shall run, and not be weary;
They shall walk, and not faint.
Isaiah 40:31

The 23rd Psalm

(For trust, confidence, courage, faith, particularly in times of distress.)

The Lord is My Shepherd, I shall not want.
He maketh me to lie down in green pastures.
He leadeth me beside the still waters.
He restoreth my Soul.
He leadeth me in the paths of righteousness
for His Name's sake.
Yea, though I walk through the

248

Valley of the Shadow of Death,
I fear no evil, for Thou art with me.
Thy rod and thy staff, they comfort me.
Thou preparest a table before me
in the presence of mine enemies.
Thou anointest my head with oil; my cup runneth over.
Surely goodness and mercy will follow me
all the days of my life
And I will dwell in the house of the Lord forever.
Amen.

Tibetan *Mantra*

(To release tensions, fears, worries; to gain peace.)

Gahtay, gahtay, para gahtay
Para sum gahtay
Bodhi swaha.

(translation)

Gone, gone, gone beyond,
Gone beyond the beyond
To the shores of enlightenment.

APPENDIX B:
SOURCES FOR *PUJAS* AND *YAGYAS*

There are two sources I recommend for *pujas* and *yagyas* done correctly and at reasonable prices. In both cases, a single ceremony for a single ES will cost about $35.00. There may be other excellent sources for quality and price. I can personally vouch for these.

1. www.puja.net is a cooperative started by my friend, Ben Collins. Ben, like me, saw the extraordinary prices charged by some providers of *pujas* and *yagyas*, and realized that they could be available to many more people if offered less expensively. Ben devised a cooperative for performing these ceremonies. I scold Ben for not providing better for his own financial needs as he arranges these services for others, but that's not who he is. Contact Ben directly at BenCollins@puja.net.

   One Puja.net service offers multiple ceremonies per month for a single fee of $51/month. Since thousands of people participate, everyone receives thousands of dollars of ceremonies during the month. Another monthly service offers more ceremonies with greater complexity for $108/mo. One year's subscription would be less than one simple ceremony from other providers.

When signing up, try to have your date, time, and place of birth available to customize the ceremony to your own energy. If your birth data is not available they will work with the energetic timing of your request so that the ceremonies are still useful.

2. www.amma.org is the contact point for Ammaji's pujas. You can learn more about the great Indian saint Amma at her website www.amma.org. Again, to arrange pujas you will need your birth data and the name of your "lunar *nakshatra*", which you can obtain from a jyotishi or from Vedic astrology software programs. Ammaji was my personal introduction to remedies for off-balance energy systems and her work is impeccable.

APPENDIX C:
MATCHING PROBLEMS TO REMEDIES

Match the symptoms to the remedy systems for a quick guide to selecting remedies:

"all or nothing" attitude	ES3	asthma	ES2
"always right"	ES5	authority issues	ES1
abscesses	ES8	blood diseases	ES2, ES3
accident-prone	ES3, ES8, ES9, ES10	bone diseases	ES1, ES7
		brain diseases	ES4
addictions	ES8, ES11	bronchitis	ES2
adversarial situations	ES3	burns	ES3
		careless	ES5
alcoholism	ES11	children, problems with	ES5
aloof	ES4	chronic illnesses	ES7
ambitionless	ES1	circulatory congestion	ES5
amoral	ES4, ES8		
anger	ES3, ES8, ES9	colic	ES2, ES8
		communication skill, lack of	ES4
anxiety	ES2, ES7, ES8	compulsive	ES8
appendicitis	ES3	concentration, lack of	ES7
argumentative	ES3		
arrogance	ES1	conflicts	ES3
arthritis	ES7	confusion	ES8, ES11

irresponsible	ES7	judgmental	ES7
irritability	ES3, ES8, ES9	pimples	ES8
		pompous	ES1
isolation	ES8, ES7, ES12	judgment, poor	ES5
		poverty	ES7
jealousy	ES1	power abuses	ES12
joint diseases	ES7	powerless	ES1
laziness	ES6, ES7	promiscuous	ES6, ES7
legal problems	ES3	psychoses	ES8, ES10
lethargy	ES1, ES4, ES7	punitive	ES3
		rashes	ES3
ligament diseases	ES7	resignation	ES7
liver diseases	ES5	restlessness	ES10
love problems	ES6	rigidity	ES7
lung diseases	ES4	ruthlessness	ES12
lymphatic congestion	ES5	self-centeredness	ES1
		sensual overindulgence	ES6, ES5
manipulation	ES12		
marital problems	ES6	sentimentality	ES6
melancholy	ES7	sexual abuses	ES12
memory problems	ES4	sexual irregularities	ES6
mental depression	ES4		
mental illnesses	ES8, ES10, ES11, ES12, ES7	shame	ES7
		shocks	ES8, ES10
		sibling problems	ES3
mentally slow	ES4	skin diseases	ES1, ES7, ES8
misfortunes	ES7		
mother problems	ES2	sorrow	ES7
muscle diseases	ES7	speculations, bad	ES5
nervousness	ES4, ES10	spiteful	ES1
neuralgia	ES1	stammering	ES4
neuroses	ES8	STDs	ES6
nightmares	ES4, ES7, ES8	stingy	ES1, ES7
		stomach troubles	ES1, ES2
obesity	ES5	stress	ES8, ES10
obsessions	ES3, ES8, ES12	stupid	ES4
		stuttering	ES4
operations	ES3	suspiciousness	ES7
ostentatious	ES1	swellings in the body	ES2
over-ambitious	ES1		
over-confidence	ES5	taste, lack of	ES6
over-indulgence	ES5	taste, loss of	ES2
overly ambitious	ES1	teacher conflicts	ES5
overly optimistic	ES5	teacher problems	ES5
over-reactive	ES2	tempted easily	ES2
over-thinking	ES4	thievery	ES4
pain (physical)	ES7	throat troubles	ES2
paralysis	ES2, ES7	timidity	ES7, ES8

APPENDIX D:
BALANCING ACTIVITIES--
A QUICK REFERENCE GUIDE

ES1/SUN

On Sundays:

> ➢ Give red flowers to a priest, government leader, or to your father.
> ➢ Give fireflies to your father.
> ➢ Red candle ritual .

ES2/MOON:

On Mondays:

> ➢ Give white flowers to a young mother.
> ➢ Give milk to a mother.
> ➢ Give milk, rice, or tapioca pudding to a shelter for women and children.
> ➢ White candle ritual.

ES3/MARS

On Tuesdays:

> ➢ Give orange (or red) flowers to a firefighter, a metalworker, a surgeon, or butcher.
> ➢ Give "red-hots" to a race-car driver.
> ➢ Throw cinnamon "red-hots" in a river or creek.
> ➢ Orange candle ritual.

ES4/MERCURY

On Wednesdays:

> ➢ Give carrots to a cat (who will eat them).
> ➢ Give a green, leafy plant to an elementary school teacher, mathematician, playground, or nursery-worker.
> ➢ Green candle ritual.

ES5/JUPITER

On Thursdays:

> ➢ Give daisies to a doe.
> ➢ Give yellow flowers to a wise teacher, university student or professor, scholar, monk, or judge.
> ➢ Give sweets to the above people, or to a charitable institution or church
> ➢ Yellow candle ritual.

ES6/VENUS

On Fridays:

> ➢ Give diamonds to divas (or rhinestones!).
> ➢ Give scented, white or pastel flowers, to a young woman, an artist, beautician, designer, art gallery.
> ➢ Scented white or pastel candle ritual.

ES7/SATURN; ES8/RAHU; ES9/KETU

On Saturdays:

> ➤ Sing the blues. Literally.
> ➤ Give black coffee, dark chocolate, dark rye bread or other dark-colored foods to the homeless.
> ➤ Give your time to elderly shut-ins.
> ➤ Feed "nuisance birds" (crows, starlings, ravens, grackles, pigeons) dark-colored food.

ES10/URANUS

Whenever you're inspired (make it several times a week):

> ➤ Give gadgets to geeks whenever you think of it.
> ➤ Wear clothing that will shock and surprise people you know.
> ➤ Give batteries or electronic gadgets to technology geeks.
> ➤ Answer the question: What DO I Really Want? (Not the same as What I DO NOT want.)

ES11/NEPTUNE

Whenever you 'feel it' (make it several times a week):

> ➤ Bring a seashell to the sea.
> ➤ Confuse a confuser.
> ➤ Take a mystic to the movies.
> ➤ Stay in the present moment. Don't make plans.
> ➤ Use essential oils.
> ➤ Go swimming or sit in a hot tub.

ES12/PLUTO

When you know you must (make it several times a week):

> ➤ Surrender your will to a higher power.
> ➤ Give away something you value to someone you believe doesn't deserve it.
> ➤ Volunteer in a hospice.
> ➤ Become obsessed with finding JOY.

BIBLIOGRAPHY

The following books are my best recommendations for those interested in remedy systems, Vedic astrology, and topics related to this book. The list includes several titles which are specific ES balancing remedies. The bibliography does not include the vast material I've referenced over 20 years of research. I wish I'd kept records of the books amassed, re: mythology encyclopedias, angelology, astronomy, astrological reference books for planetary correspondences, and other resources used to develop the ES database over two decades. The list below is most functional for the general reader. I hope it is useful for you.

The Greatness of Saturn by Robert Svoboda. Lotus Press, 1997.
> In addition to being a balancing activity in and of itself, Svoboda's book contains an excellent table of energy remedies which was the seed idea for this book. Svoboda's knowledge of the subject is profound and his suggestions are brilliant.

Light on Life: An Introduction to the Astrology of India by Hart de Fouw and Robert Svoboda. South Asia Books, 1996.
> This is arguably THE best book for westerners who are serious about learning Vedic astrology. Densely packed with techniques and background information. If you know everything in this book you will be an excellent Jyotishi.

Path of Light, V1 — Introduction to Vedic Astrology; V2 — The Domains of Life by James Kelleher. Ahimsa Press, 2006.
Thorough and very readable, this ties for first place as the best book for westerners who want to learn Vedic astrology. Although not as encyclopedic or as densely packed as de Fouw's and Svoboda's book, it is easier to follow.

Mantra Yoga and Primal Sound: The Secret of Seed (Bija) Mantras by David Frawley. Lotus Press, 2010.
For more information on *mantras*, and for many more *mantras*, you can't do better than this book.

Healing Mantras: Using Sound Affirmations for Personal Power, Creativity and Healing by Thomas Ashley-Farrand.
Wellspring/Ballantine, 1999.
More excellent background information and *mantras* for healing your life.

Healing Mantras (Audio CD) by Thomas Ashley-Farrand. Sounds True, 2000.
So you can HEAR the *mantras*. Just playing the CD will activate their energy systems in your vibrational field. Learning them will do even more.

The Planets Within: The Astrological Psychology of Marcilio Ficino by Thomas Moore. Lindesfarne Books, 1990.
Shows how medieval western thought echoed the more ancient Vedic principles of balancing energy systems.

Making the Gods Work For You: The Astrological Language of the Psyche by Caroline Casey. Three Rivers Press, 1999.
Modern western thinking on balancing energy systems. Clever, witty, fun.

Turning the Tables: A Mitigation Manual by Barbara Cameron.
American Federation of Astrologers (AFA) 1984.
Another western view on planetary remedies, this one full of detail. Her use of the term "Rahu" for the Moon's north node tells us she used Vedic systems for source material.

Remedial Measures in Astrology by Dr. Gouri Shankar Kapoor. South Asia Books, 1997.

Thorough overview of traditional Indian methods for balancing energy systems.

Vedic Remedies in Astrology by Sanjay Rath. Sagar Publications, 2002.
Another excellent overview of traditional Indian balancing methods.

Lal Kitab This ancient Indian text has been translated from Urdu many times over the centuries and many different editions are available. My copy is:
Astrology and Remedies of Lal Kitab: Easy and Effective Inexpensive Remedial Measures by D.P. Saxena. Ranjan Publications, 1997.
This is a richly annotated version of the classic Indian guide to astrological remedies. However the remedies are more culturally suited to India than to the contemporary western world.

Cosmos and Psyche: Intimations of a New World View by Richard Tarnas, Ph.D. Viking Press, 2006.
As a university professor, professional historian, astrologer, and genius, Tarnas has demonstrated how patterns in all areas of human endeavor and throughout recorded history correspond to the geometric patterns of planets in the sky. This book will teach you history and a profoundly new understanding of the world, through archetypal planetary energies. The subtitle *"Intimations of a New World View"* is highly significant.

Healing Stories Bibliography

Goodnight Moon (book and CD) by Margaret Wise Brown. Harper Festival, 2006.
This classic children's book is a beloved memory for many adults. Reading it is a remedy for ES2/Moon.

Don Quijote by Miguel de Cervantes, or the 1965 musical *Man From La Mancha* are remedies for ES4/Mercury.

Horton Hatches the Egg, by Dr. Seuss. Random House Books for Young Readers, 2004. And *Horton Hears a Who,* by Dr. Seuss. Harper Collins Children's Books, 2012
These classic children's' books capture the essence of ES5/Jupiter, and offer a remedy for ES5. Read them aloud to children.

The Ugly Duckling, the fairy tale by Hans Christian Anderson are remedies for ES5/Jupiter. Read it aloud to a child, or read to yourself.

Any of the stories about *Babar, the Elephant,* by Jean or Lauren de Brunhoff. This is a lovely series of children's books about suitable as a remedy for ES5/Jupiter.

The Horse Whisperer, by Nicholas Evans. Dell Reprint Edition, 2011. Reading this is a remedy for ES6/Venus.

Black Beauty, by Anna Sewell. Simon and Brown (reprint) 2011. Another reading remedy for ES6/Venus.

Autobiography of a Yogi, by Paramahansa Yogananda. Self Realization Fellowship, 2000.
> Reading this classic book can serve as remedies for ES5/Jupiter and ES11/Neptune.

The Greatness of Saturn (see above) is a classic remedy for ES7/Saturn.

The Book of Job from the *Old Testament* is another classic ES7/Saturn remedy.

J.B.: A Play in Verse by Archibald MacLeish. Houghton Mifflin, 1989.
This won a Pulitzer in 1959 and a Tony for best play. It is a 20th century retelling of the story of Job, and an excellent ES7/Saturn remedy.

Shantaram (autobiographical novel) by Gregory David Roberts. St. Martins Griffin, 2005.
> Reading this book is a balancing activity for ES7/Saturn; ES8/Rahu, ES10/Uranus, ES11/Neptune, and ES12/Pluto. Besides that, it's a fabulous and memorable epic novel, brilliantly written and offering a panoramic view of life in India through the eyes of a westerner. I especially recommend the CDs of this book:

Shantaram by Gregory David Roberts, read by Humphrey Bower. Audiofile, 2006.
> Bower has a great voice and a gift for accents, and you will recognize characters by his brilliant use of both. (I've listened to the 35-CD set four times.)

ॐ

INDEX

O

P

ACKNOWLEDGMENTS

This book would not have been possible without the wisdom of my teachers. The errors are entirely my own. I give thanks to K.N. Rao for his educational leadership, for pointing out the non-denominational nature of Vedic remedies and insisting on the efficacy of charity and devotion. Thanks also to Robert Svoboda for his book, **_The Greatness of Saturn,_** which planted the seed for this book; to Hart de Fouw for his brilliant teaching and for sharing his experiences with remedies; and to my teacher, Marc Boney, the U.S. lineage-holder for K.N. Rao. Warm thanks to my friend and fellow student Ben Collins, for whom helping people is a life path. Finally, many thanks go to my wonderful clients and students who teach me in each and every session.

I am overwhelmed with gratitude to friends whose generous assistance in the production of this book was essential. This includes my sister, Paula Gabbard, for logo art; Jim Hennum for photography; and Christine Matzke for graphics and design assistance. Most especially, EA Campbell, Margarette Kaylor, Barbara McLeod and Paula Wilson contributed eagle eyes and many grueling hours for copy and content editing. Remaining mistakes are my fault.

Thanks always to the power of divine grace, which lifts me up when I'm in need.

Photo by Jim Hennum

ABOUT THE AUTHOR

Anne Beversdorf is a practitioner of Vedic and western astrology. Since 1993 her internationally published articles and workshops have brought her a worldwide clientele. Her award-winning e-newsletter and website (www.stariel.com) contain additional educational material.

Anne has owned an educational software company, taught at Indiana University and San Diego State University, consulted with Fortune 100 companies, and set up several specialized libraries prior to beginning her astrological practice. She received her B.A., *magna cum laude,* from the University of Texas at Austin, and an M.L.S. from Indiana University, Bloomington. She has been honored in Marquis' Who's Who in America, and Who's Who in the World for her business and astrological practices.

Additionally, Anne is a respected fiber artist, creating detailed miniature tapestries of silk and jewels. The art can be viewed at www.sacred-threads.com and appears in this book, as well as in numerous galleries.

Anne lives in the Texas Hill Country with her two beloved pups. She can be reached by email at anne@ stariel.com.

Manufactured by Amazon.ca
Bolton, ON